Financial Freedom Secrets

David Shepherd

Financial Freedom Secrets

Investing Disclaimer

There is always a risk in investing. This book contains MY strategy and you should always use a financial advisor for your unique situation. Here is my legal disclaimer about stock investing:

Past performance is not indicative of future results. I do not guarantee any specific outcome or profit. You should be aware of the real risk of loss in following any strategy or investment discussed in this book. Strategies or investments discussed may fluctuate in price or value. Investors may get back less than invested. Investments or strategies mentioned in this book may not be suitable for you. This material does not take into account your particular investment objectives, financial situation or needs and is not intended as recommendations appropriate for you. You must make an independent decision regarding investments or strategies mentioned in this book. Before acting on information in this book, you should consider whether it is suitable for your particular circumstances and strongly consider seeking advice from your own financial or investment adviser.

Bonus Materials

I've created a bonus resource site where you can access spreadsheets, frameworks, and more. This will help you succeed so I highly suggest signing up for it now. Inside you'll find all the resources organized by each of the secrets in this book making it super easy to use! I'll be adding more content over time so make sure you get free instant access right now!

Visit the following link to get free access to your Financial Freedom Secrets bonus materials now:

https://moneybadass.teachable.com/courses/financial-freedom-secrets

Dedicated To

Dedicated to my amazing wife who has supported me on my crazy adventure and our awesome four kids who make our lives very entertaining and fun.

This ones for you Krista, Hayden, Eden, Rylie, and Blake!

Contents

Introduction

Section One:
Foundations

Contents

Section Two: Take Control

Section Three: Wealth

Contents

Introduction

Imagine that you had enough income coming in each month from your investments that you never had to work a 9-5 job again.

Imagine that you had the ability to travel the world whenever you wanted to without financial stress.

Imagine that your money was running on autopilot for you day and night.

Imagine being able to spend time with your friends and family on your own terms. Not your bosses.

Imagine that you no longer had to stress about having enough money for your bills and no longer had to worry about paying off debt.

That is the life of financial freedom.

You don't have to imagine it. YOU can live that life by taking the right steps with your money NOW.

Democratizing Financial Knowledge

The secrets I'm about to tell you are the key to reaching financial freedom. The secrets of the wealthiest people in America. All you have to do is take action and implement every one of these secrets in your own life and you will become wealthier than you ever thought possible.

For way too long this information has been too hard for the average person to learn. Only the wealthy had access by paying for accountants, financial advisors, and investment managers. No more. I'm breaking down the secrets of the wealthy in easy to understand frameworks that anyone can implement in their own financial lives.

Introduction

This book is designed to be all actionable advice. You won't find pages of fluff. You're going to get to the point actionable advice that you can implement in your own life today. No fluff, no BS, to the point, actionable advice.

Are you ready? Let's do this.

Section One: Foundations

This section contains the foundational secrets to reaching financial freedom. You need to understand and implement these secrets first before moving to Section 2. These foundational secrets will make working through the secrets in Section 2 and 3 much easier so don't skip these steps.

In Secret #1 you will learn where you are on the Financial Freedom Pyramid.

Next, in Secret #2, you'll discover the Financial Freedom Roadmap you'll need to follow to reach financial freedom.

In Secret #3, you'll also learn how to find your Financial Freedom Number so you'll know exactly how much money you will need to reach financial freedom. I'll even show you some tricks to get it as low as possible and how to get there even faster.

Finally, in Secret #4, you're going to learn how to implement a Money Discovery which will help you pull together all of your financial details. This will be a huge help in the later secrets.

Are you ready? Let's get started now with Secret #1.

Secret #1 - Financial Freedom Pyramid

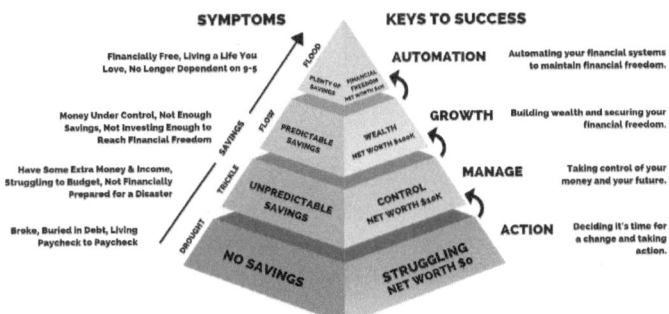

Reaching financial freedom is a journey. It's not immediate. It's not going to happen by tomorrow and it's not for everyone. If it was easy and everyone knew how to do it, everyone would have reached financial freedom by now.

The first secret you need to understand is the Financial Freedom Pyramid. Everyone is somewhere on the Financial Freedom Pyramid whether they know it or not. Most people are at the bottom of the pyramid and as you move up the pyramid you will find less and less people, because most people don't understand how to climb the pyramid.

Unfortunately, most people don't even realize the Financial Freedom Pyramid exists so they'll be stuck at the bottom for the rest of their life. Lucky for you, I'm about to tell you how the Financial Freedom Pyramid works and show you exactly how you can climb the pyramid. Plus I'll show you how to do it as fast as possible throughout the secrets in this book.

There are four stages to the Financial Freedom Pyramid. No matter where you are on the Financial Freedom

Pyramid today the secrets in this books will help you reach the next stage and ultimately financial freedom at the top.

Stage 1

This is the bottom of the pyramid. This where most people are and will be for the rest of their lives unless they learn and take action.

In this stage you are consistently broke, buried in debt, and living paycheck to paycheck. Your savings rate is a drought and you have very little saved. You're only one emergency away from disaster. You are struggling with day to day expenses and have a negative or nearly $0 net worth.

If you are in this stage, you have to decide on your own that it is time to start taking action on your money and begin implementing the secrets within this book in your life immediately. This is the only way you can avoid financial disaster and end the cycle of struggling.

I'm going to show the secrets you need to know to get out of this stage and move up the Financial Freedom Pyramid to Stage 2.

Stage 2

This is the next stage up the Financial Freedom Pyramid. There are a lot of people in this tier but, less people than Stage 1.

In this stage you have some extra money from your income left over each month to spend or save, but you struggling to budget your money properly. You're not truly prepared for an emergency. Your savings rate is a trickle and unpredictable at best. Your net worth is $10,000 or more.

If you are in this stage, you need to take control of your money to move up the Financial Freedom Pyramid. You need to get a clear picture of your finances, manage your money better, review your bills, and get out of debt.

The secrets in Section 2 of this book will help you move to Stage 3 of the Financial Freedom Pyramid.

Stage 3

The next stage up the Financial Freedom Pyramid is even smaller than Stage 2. Many people will never reach this stage in their lifetimes because they don't understand the secrets of financial freedom.

If you are in this stage, you will have your money under control. You'll have a predictable and steady flow of savings. You'll have a net worth of at least $100,000 and you'll be beginning to build some real wealth.

However, you most likely are not investing your savings well enough to reach financial freedom as fast as possible and move up to Stage 4 of the Financial Freedom

Pyramid. You're probably not maximizing your income streams and haven't automated your money.

If you are in this stage you are very close to financial freedom, but you will need to invest your money the right way to secure financial freedom as fast as possible and reach Stage 4 of the Financial Freedom Pyramid.

The secrets in Section 3 of this book will help you to close the gap and reach Stage 4 of the Financial Freedom Pyramid as quickly as possible.

Stage 4

This is the final stage of the Financial Freedom Pyramid. This stage has the smallest amount of people, because very few people reach financial freedom.

If you've hit this stage, you've reached financial freedom. You're living a life you love and you are no longer dependent on a 9-5 job if you don't want one. You'll have a flood of savings invested well and multiple income streams that can maintain your lifestyle for the rest of your life.

In you are in this stage, you've reached the ultimate goal but, I'm still going to help you stay in this stage by showing you the secrets to invest your money the right way and automate your money so you can stay in Stage 4 for the rest of your life on autopilot.

It Doesn't Matter What Stage You Are In Today

It doesn't matter what stage you are in today. What matters is where you are going in the future and that is to Stage 4.

You now know the secret of the Financial Freedom Pyramid. Now it's time to learn the secrets to climb the Financial Freedom Pyramid as fast as possible.

Secret #1 - Financial Freedom Pyramid

Are you ready to climb the Financial Freedom Pyramid?
On to Secret #2.

Secret #2 - Financial Freedom Roadmap

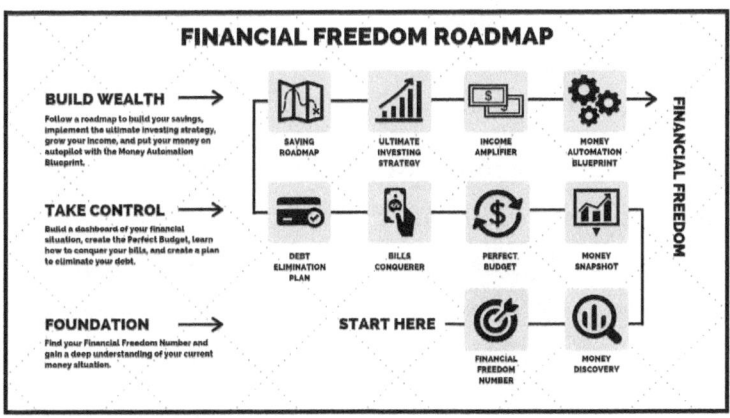

To reach financial freedom you don't create a budget. You don't save 15% of your money. You don't open a 401k.

Secret #2 - Financial Freedom Roadmap

You follow a system. I'm going to show you that system. That system is Secret #2. It's called the Financial Freedom Roadmap.

Way too often I'll talk to people who think they just need to invest a little more in their 401k or open a Roth IRA so they can reach financial freedom and retire before they're too old to enjoy it. That's not how it works.

Nearly every wealthy person in the world (who didn't inherit their money) have one way or another gone down this same roadmap in their life. They've taken a series of steps in the right order to take total control of their money and build wealth.

To reach financial freedom you have to follow this roadmap step-by-step. Don't try to skip steps or jump around. That will just slow you down and possibly cause you to fail altogether. Follow the system. Follow every step of the way. In order. If you do this, you will become wealthy. Wealthier then you ever thought possible.

The Financial Freedom Roadmap is challenging, but worth it. Each step will take you one stop closer to

Financial Freedom. I'm going to walk you through each section and secret of the Financial Freedom Roadmap throughout this book. For now, I'm going to give you that 10,000 foot view of the Financial Freedom Roadmap right now.

Section 1 - Foundations

The first section of the Financial Freedom Roadmap is Foundations. This is the foundational secrets that you need to implement first. Without these secrets you'll never be able to truly succeed in the Financial Freedom Roadmap. Don't skip it. Learn it and it will make the rest of the secrets so much easier to implement.

Secret #3 - Financial Freedom Number

When you begin your journey to financial freedom you will need to find out what your Financial Freedom Number is. This is your goal. This is where you are going and this is where the Financial Freedom Roadmap is taking you. You will discover exactly how much money you will need to be able to reach a life of financial freedom.

Secret #4 - Money Discovery

You're not going to make much progress if you don't understand your entire financial picture. That is what a Money Discovery is for. You need to know all the details of your money. You need to know where it is at, what's coming in, what's going out, etc. The Money Discovery will help you figure all that out in the quickest and easiest way possible.

Section 2 - Take Control

Once you understand and have implemented the Foundational secrets you will be ready to begin Section 2 and take control of your money. In Section 2 - Take Control you will learn the secrets to manage your money. No more being bullied by lenders and companies. YOU control your money, not them. Learn the secrets to take control of your money like never before.

Secret #5 - Money Snapshot

It's very powerful to have all of your finances broken down to a dashboard that you can quickly glance over and understand your total financial position. That's power over your money and that's what I call a Money Snapshot. In addition to tracking your money, you MUST know your net worth. No, it's not some financial term for billionaires. It condenses your entire financial health into one number.

You must always know your net worth. You'll learn how to do all of this in the Money Snapshot.

Secret #6 - Perfect Budget

Budgets don't have to be a pain. The secret is creating a budget that works for you. That is the Perfect Budget and it is a requirement to reach financial freedom. It would be really difficult to truly control your money without a budget. You MUST create a budget and you MUST own it. You need to know how much money is coming in and where it is going every day. The Perfect Budget will show you how to create an efficient and easy to use budget.

Secret #7 - Bills Conquerer

Bills suck. That's why you need to be in total control of them. At first that Netflix subscription doesn't seem so bad and then you add on Spotify. Next you add a new Verizon plan to your bills. Don't forget your subsidized phone payments. That's how bills add up like little leeches on your bank account. You MUST take control and eliminate all those leaches sucking on your bank account. You have to minimize those bills down to only what you need and truly want. The Bills Conquerer will help you do exactly that.

Secret #8 - Debt Elimination Plan

Debt is a drain on our generation. It's shoved down our throats from the day we turn 18 and that is just plain wrong. Credit cards, student loans, car loans, it's never ending. You CANNOT fall for that. You HAVE TO pay down that debt in the fastest and most automated way possible. You will never build wealth and reach financial freedom until you eliminate your debt. The Debt Elimination Plan is an easy and automated system to eliminate your debt for good.

Section 3 - Wealth

The final section called Wealth will give you the secrets to build wealth and turn your dream of reaching financial freedom into reality. Within these secrets you will learn how much to save, how to invest those savings, how to amplify your income, and automate your money.

Secret #9 - Saving Roadmap

Saving money is critical to reaching financial freedom. If you don't save enough money, you're living paycheck to paycheck and that's a terrible way to live. One emergency and you're struggling to pay the bills. You'll fall back into relying on the old credit card to get by which just buries you further into debt. You CANNOT live that way. I'll show you how much you need to be saving to avoid the paycheck to paycheck cycle.

Secret #10 - Ultimate Investing Strategy

Investing has been overcomplicated by TV gurus and day traders who have attempted to make us believe that you need to rely on others to invest your money. Did they mention they take a fee for that? Of course not. The Ultimate Investing Strategy will show you a simple but effective strategy that has beat 95% of financial advisors, hedge fund managers, and investing gurus out there.

Secret #11 - Income Amplifier

Wealthy people don't rely only on a 9-5 to earn money. They have multiple income streams. In the Income Amplifier I'll show you the income streams that the rich are using to get rich. You'll learn how to amplify your 9-5 income and build new income streams that will help you reach financial freedom much faster than you thought possible.

Secret #12 - Money Automation Blueprint

Imagine that you have a personal assistant handling nearly everything regarding your money. Your bills are automatically paid, your debt is being paid down, your money is being invested all while you do the things you love. Well, you don't have to imagine it, it's possible with technology and the Money Automation Blueprint will teach you how to do just that. I'll help you setup your own automation system for your money so your Financial Freedom Roadmap is running on autopilot while you climb the Financial Freedom Pyramid.

The Financial Freedom Roadmap Is Not For Everyone

The Financial Freedom Road takes time and action. Not everyone has the passion, the grit, and the willpower to do it. Don't be one of them. You bought this book to transform your life and if you are willing to do the work and implement these secrets in your own life, you will succeed.

The transformation from being broke and feeling helpless to financial freedom is one of the most satisfying and life fulfilling journeys you can take. Don't let another day pass by without doing something about it! Start right now with Secret #3 - Financial Freedom Number.

Secret #3 - Financial Freedom Number

No matter where your finances are today the very first step to financial freedom is to find your Financial Freedom Number. You have to know your Financial Freedom Number first, otherwise you are just aimlessly trying to resolve your money problems with no end goal to work towards.

What is a Financial Freedom Number? It's the amount of money you need to never work again if you choose. It's the amount of money you need to no longer be dependent on anyone else for your own life. When you have that much money you have hit financial freedom.

The 4% Rule

There's a financial rule that's called the 4% rule. Now, I don't want to bore you and waste your time so I'm going to summarize it up for you very quickly.

Financial researchers have found that, at retirement, you can safely withdraw 4% of your retirement money without running out of money based on historical financial data. In other words, if you have enough money that you could withdraw 4% of it a year safely and live off of it, you've hit financial freedom.

I believe that number is too conservative, but it's a great starting point. I'll show you how we can adjust that later, but first, let's find out what your Financial Freedom Number is using the 4% rule for now.

How To Find Your Financial Freedom Number

To find your Financial Freedom Number you'll first need to determine how much money you will need to pay your expenses each month. So sit down, grab a paper and pencil, or a spreadsheet and let's figure out everything you have to spend money on each month.

I've listed some monthly expenses you may have below. For anything else put it in the "Other" section. At the end of the list total up your monthly expenses.

Monthly Expenses:

- Mortgage / Rent: $
- Car Payments: $
- Loan Payments: $

- Credit Card Payments: $
- Electricity: $
- Water: $
- Internet: $
- Cable TV: $
- Cell Phone: $
- Fuel: $
- Health Care: $
- Entertainment: $
- Insurance: $
- Eating Out: $
- Clothing: $
- Savings: $
- Other: $
- Other: $
- Other: $
- Other: $
- Other: $
- Other: $
- Other: $

Secret #3 - Financial Freedom Number

Total Monthly Expenses: $

There is no wrong answer. Some people can live off of $1,000 per month. Others may live off of $5,000 per month or even more.

Now take your Total Monthly Expenses and multiply it by 300.

My Financial Freedom Number = Total Monthly Expenses x 300

That's it, that is your Financial Freedom Number. That is how you calculate your Financial Freedom Number using the 4% Rule. Now, I feel like the 4% Rule is conservative and could be adjusted so I'll show you how you can adjust your Financial Freedom Number.

Adjusting Your Financial Freedom Number

You can also get your Financial Freedom Number using a different formula:

Financial Freedom Number = (Total Monthly Expenses x 12) / .04

This is your total annual expenses divided by .04 for the 4% rule. Earlier I had said that financial researchers have found that 4% is a safe amount to pull from your retirement account, but what if we're more aggressive?

We're millennials, we can always pick up side hustles, go back to work if needed, and we can invest much more aggressively than someone who is 65.

Secret #3 - Financial Freedom Number

Let's say you believe you can safely pull 5% from your Financial Freedom money. All you have to do is adjust the formula:

Financial Freedom Number = (Total Monthly Expenses x 12) / .05

The last number is the percentage, adjust the number to what makes sense for you and your life. Maybe you still want to run a small business or side hustle even after you reach financial freedom. You can withdraw more than 4% safely.

What if you can consistently get a 10% return or more on your investments rather than the typical 7%? You can withdraw more than 4% safely.

I'll show you an example. Let's say your monthly expenses are $2,500. I'll run the calculations below to show you how the Financial Freedom Number goes down as you can withdraw more:

-   (2,500 x 12)) / .04 = $750,000

- (2,500 x 12)) / .05 = $600,000
- (2,500 x 12)) / .06 = $500,000
- (2,500 x 12)) / .07 = $428,571
- (2,500 x 12)) / .08 = $375,000
- (2,500 x 12)) / .09 = $333,333
- (2,500 x 12)) / .10 = $300,000

The more you can safely withdraw the lower your number will go.

Financial Freedom Number Levers

There are certain "levers" you can pull in your finances to make the Financial Freedom number smaller which will help you reach that number even faster.

Monthly Expenses

The amount of your monthly expenses play a big role in your Financial Freedom Number. Let's say you are able to reduce your monthly expenses after reviewing your bills and eliminating your debt. That will reduce your Financial Freedom Number as well.

For example, let's run through the Financial Freedom Number with 4 different Monthly Expenses:

- (2,500 x 12) / .04 = $750,000
- (2,000 x 12) / .04 = $600,000
- (1,500 x 12) / .04 = $450,000
- (1,000 x 12) / .04 = $300,000

In the Bills Conquerer and Debt Elimination Plan secrets, I'll show you how you can reduce your monthly expenses efficiently.

Monthly Savings

Your monthly savings rate also plays a big part in how fast you will reach your Financial Freedom Number. If you're only saving 5% of your income it's going to take longer than if you were saving 25% of your income to reach your Financial Freedom Number.

Monthly Income

The more money you make, the more you can save, thus decreasing the amount of time it will take to reach your Financial Freedom Number.

In the Income Amplifier Secret I'll show you how you can increase your 9-5 income and how to add income streams to help you reach your Financial Freedom Number even faster.

Return On Investment

Historical returns in the stock market have been about 7% over time, but what if you could increase your returns to 10%, 15%, or even more?

In the Ultimate Investing Strategy secret I'll show you how I've earned double digit returns each year and beat the returns of 95% of hedge fudge managers, mutual fund managers, and financial advisors.

By increasing the returns on your investments, you'll be able to grow your financial freedom money faster and increase the amount of money you can safely withdraw from your Financial Freedom money. This will help you reduce your Financial Freedom Number and get there even faster.

Action Steps

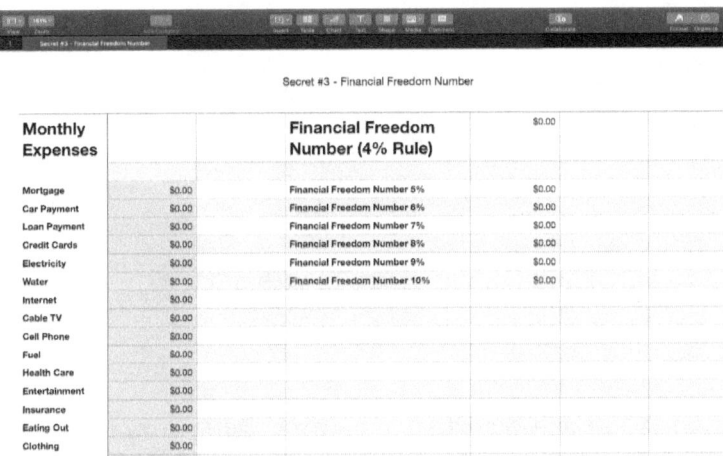

If you haven't already, sit down, take the time, and calculate your Financial Freedom Number. You'll find a spreadsheet that will make it even easier on the bonus materials site! Now it's time to make this happen:

- Calculate your Financial Freedom Number

Secret #4 - Money Discovery

You're probably saying to yourself, "what is a Money Discovery?"

Imagine you are a detective at a crime scene. You can't just jump in and start arresting people without analyzing the situation. You don't even know who to question or what to ask. The first step is to take photos, search for fingerprints, and collect evidence. You need to gather all the info you can before you can begin getting into the details.

Money is the same way. The first step to working on your money is to gather all the info before you even begin to consider budgeting, bills, and investing. Wealthy people have been doing this (often with their accountant or financial advisor) to help them gain a total financial picture of their money before making decisions or taking financial actions for years.

During the Money Discovery you'll dig into your finances and gather all the information you will need to implement the rest of the secrets in this book. Don't skip it. You will need to know this information. Grab a pen / paper or open a spreadsheet on your computer and follow along.

Step 1 - List Out All Your Monthly Income

First step, let's gather all of your income information. This is one of the easiest parts of the Money Discovery because I bet you know all about the money you have coming in don't you? Who doesn't?

To help you get rolling, here are some examples that may apply to you:

- Job Paycheck
- Side Hustle Income
- Rental Property Income
- Child Support
- Spousal Support
- Veteran Income
- Social Security
- Disability Income

There's plenty more out there. Just think of anywhere your money comes from monthly. List out each source and the monthly amount you get from that income.

Here is an example:

- Job Paycheck: $3,800 Per Month

If it varies, it's better to estimate on the low end rather than the high end. For a Money Discovery just focus on your net income. That basically means what you take home or what is deposited into your bank account. Forget about gross income which is what you get before everything is taken out like taxes and health insurance. That's not needed for now.

Step 2 - List Out All Your Monthly Bills And Expenses

Now, let's talk about where your money is going. This is a huge eye opener for most people. A lot of times we feel overwhelmed with our financial situation and begin to ignore our finances. You have to be aware of your financial situation at all times. That's the whole point of a Money Discovery. You are going to understand everything about your money. You'll know what's going in, what's going out, and much more.

This step is where you get a handle on your money that is going out each month. I want you to list out all of your monthly expenses. Sit down and really think about everything you spend money on monthly. You probably already have most of this information from calculating your Financial Freedom Number. It will be helpful if you pull up your transaction history from your bank account from the last few months and review each transaction.

To get you started, here is a list of possible categories of expenses you may have:

- Mortgage
- Home Insurance
- Home Maintenance
- Real Estate Taxes
- Water
- Electric
- Internet
- Fuel
- Car Insurance
- Car Maintenance
- Phone
- Groceries
- Investing

- Home Design
- Clothing
- Medical
- Gifts
- Vacation
- Cool Stuff
- Dining Out
- Adventure

Maybe you have more expenses than the ones I listed out above. If you do, put them on your list. Anything you spend money on should fall into some category on your list. Hopefully this will give you a "a ha" moment once you realize where all of your money is going to.

Step 3 - List Out All Your Bank Accounts

This step will be a bit easier. Think of all your bank accounts. Let's get a handle on everywhere you have money right now. Do you have checking accounts? Do you have a savings account? Do you have any joint accounts? List them out on your paper or spreadsheet. Sometimes people will have old accounts they haven't checked on in a while. Try to think of any bank accounts you haven't used in a while as well.

Here are some possible accounts you may have:

- Checking Account
- Savings Account
- Health Savings Account
- Joint Account
- Paypal Account

Any other cash or bank accounts? List them out.

Step 4 - List Out All Your Debts

Do you have any debt accounts? If don't have any, keep on moving to the next section. Congrats by the way, that's awesome! Most likely, you do have some debts though. Most people have debt today. If you've been ignoring that debt it's now time to stare it in the face and take the first step to tackling that debt full on. Pull up that spreadsheet again or grab your paper and fill in every debt account you can think of.

Here are some common debts that people have:

- Mortgage
- Rental Property Mortgage
- Car Loans
- Student Loans
- Misc Vehicle Loans like RV's, Motorcycles, and Off Road Vehicles
- Lines of Credit

- Credit Cards
- Home Equity

If I missed a debt that you have make sure to add it to the list as well.

Step 5 - List Out All Your Physical Assets

We're moving right along. Now, let's list out all your physical assets. This is anything physical you own that has value. Lots of items you own probably have some value, but for Money Discovery purposes it's best to focus on high priced items like your house or cars.

Here are some examples of physical assets you may have:

- House
- Rental Property

- Car
- Misc Vehicle Loans like RV's, Motorcycles, and Off Road Vehicles

Enter each of your physical assets into your spreadsheet or write them down on your paper.

Step 6 - List Out All Your Investments

Now, let's look at your investments. Think of every investment account you have. If you've worked at several companies over the years do you have multiple retirement accounts? Do you have private investment accounts like a Roth IRA or Robinhood stock trading account?

Here is a list of some example investment accounts to get you started:

- 401K's
- Roth 401K's

- Roth IRA's

- Traditional IRA's

- 529 Plan

- Stock investment accounts like Robinhood

- App investment accounts like Stash

Finish up your spreadsheet or paper Money Discovery with every investment you can think of.

Step 7 - List Out Your Financial Goals

Lastly, let's focus on the fun stuff. What do you want to do with your money? Remember, money is just a tool to help you achieve want you want in life. What do you want and need in life? There is where you get to have some fun. What do you ultimately want to do with your money? Take some time and think about what goals you want to save for.

Here are just a few ideas:

- Vacations
- New cars
- Down payment on a house

List them by total amount and how much you would need to save monthly to hit your final goal in the time frame you set. To calculate how money you would need to save per month you can use this formula:

Monthly Amount = Total Amount / Years / 12

What Do I Do With My Money Discovery?

Once you've got everything listed out, you have the whole picture of your finances. This should be a mind opening experience if you haven't been tracking your money in the past. Now you know where all of money is, how much you have, how much you owe, and where you want to go with your money.

This is good to see and know, but this is only a first step. This is a launching point to the next secrets. From here you can now begin to build a budget, track your net worth, pay down your debt, increase your income, reduce your expenses, etc. The list goes on and on.

Remember, taking control of your money is a journey, but you don't need to focus on the whole journey. Just one step at a time and now you've taken a solid step further on the journey. Start with the first step, then the next, and so on. In the end you'll get there and you'll be happy you did.

Let's wrap up with the actions steps you need to take.

Action Steps

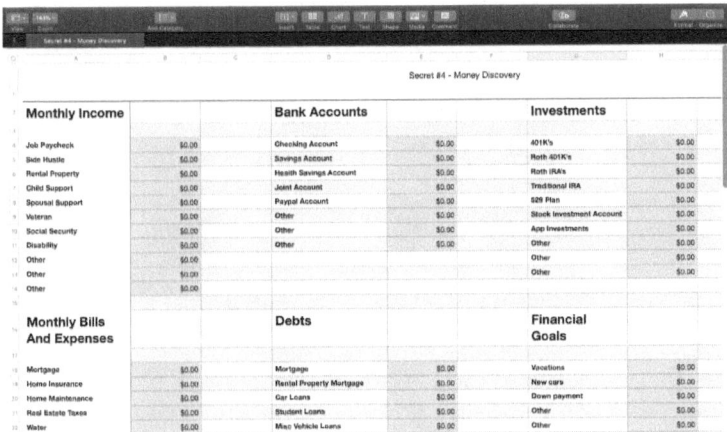

You'll find a spreadsheet that will make it even easier on the bonus materials site!

- List out all of your monthly income

- List out all of your monthly expenses

- List out all of your bank accounts

- List out all of your debt accounts

- List out all of your physical assets

Secret #4 - Money Discovery

- List out all of your investment accounts
- List out all of your financial goals

Section Two: Take Control

By now you should understand and have implemented the Foundational Secrets within your personal finances. Next, I'm going to show you how to take total control over your money with 4 new secrets.

First, in Secret #5, I'll show you how to create a Money Snapshot. This is like a financial dashboard for your life. A personal balance sheet to show you at a glance where your finances stand.

Next, in Secret #6, you'll learn how to create the Perfect Budget. This is a budget that is easy to use, yet gives you total control over your money. This will make reaching financial freedom so much easier and allow you to spend money guilt free.

Then, you'll learn how to take control of your bills in Secret #7 with the Bills Conquerer. Bills area like little leaches on your bank account. I'll show you how to review and eliminate the ones you really don't need while focusing on the ones you do want.

Finally, in Secret #8, we'll tackle and conquer your debt with the Debt Elimination Plan. Debt is ruining millennials chances at reaching financial freedom, but I'll show you how to stop debt for good in your own life.

Let's get started with Secret #5.

Secret #5 - Money Snapshot

I'm going to show you how to create a Money Snapshot. We're going to take everything you pulled together in your Money Discovery and create a Money Snapshot with it.

A lot of people I've talked to believe money is just a budget and investing. No, there is way more to money than that. I graduated with a bachelors degree in accounting… Yes, I'm that kind of guy. I had to learn all about business finances in college. This may be boring, but just give me a few sentences to explain how your money relates to business finances.

To run a business there are two main financial reports you have to understand. They are the balance statement and the income statement. That may sound like a bunch of business jargon totally unrelated to your money, but they are very similar to what you need in your personal finances to take control of your money.

An income statement is very similar to the typical personal budget in personal finances and the balance statement is very similar to what I call a Money Snapshot. That's what I'm going to show you how to do. We're going to create a Money Snapshot just like a business creates a balance sheet.

You're probably wondering why?

Well, it gives you an incredible understanding of your money and being aware of your money gives you control over your money. That's how you need to manage your money if you want to reach financial freedom.

Best of all, it organizes your money into a simple format that you can quickly glance over and understand your total financial picture. It's kinda like a dashboard for your money.

How to Create Your Money Snapshot

At this point, you should have already completed your Money Discovery. If not, go back and do it. There's no way to continue with this secret without completing your Money Discovery.

Once you're done with the Money Discovery, pull up a spreadsheet, or grab a pencil and paper and let's get started. At the top of the page add, "Assets." Now we are going to list out all of your assets.

Bank Accounts

First up is your bank accounts. Let's get a handle on everywhere you have money right now.

Under Assets, title this section, "Bank Accounts."

This is more or less going to be filling in the blanks because you already did most of the hard work in the Money Discovery. So, pull out your Money Discovery and list out all your bank accounts and the current balances.

At the end of the Bank Accounts list add up all your bank accounts to get a "Total."

Physical Assets

We are moving right along. Now let's list out all your physical assets. This is anything physical you own that has value.

Under Assets, title this section, "Physical Assets."

You've probably already listed them in your Money Discovery so enter those assets into the Money Snapshot under Physical Assets along with their current value. If you don't know how much they are worth, there are sites that can give you an estimated value. Zillow is great for getting an estimate of any real estate you own and KBB is great for getting an estimate of your vehicle values.

At the end of the Physical Assets list add up all your physical assets to get a "Total."

Investments

Next, let's take a look at your investments.

Under Assets, title this section, "Investments."

Pull out your Money Discovery and make sure you have every investment account listed. List out every investment account you have under investments section of your Money Snapshot along with their current values.

At the end of the investments list add up all your investments to get a "Total."

Now that you have all of your assets listed, add up the totals of your bank accounts, physical assets, and investments. At the end of your Assets list add a line for "Total Assets." and enter the amount there.

Debt

Now, we're switching from assets to debt. Start a new column and at the top of the page add, "Debt." We are going to list out all of your debt.

Use your Money Discovery again to fill in all of your debt accounts and the amount you currently owe for each of them.

At the end of the debt list add up all your debt to get a "Total Debt."

Let's move to final piece of the Money Snapshot, your Net Worth.

How To Find Your Net Worth

By now you've got a pretty full page and your Money Snapshot is beginning to come together. Now that you have completed your assets and debt, it's time to figure out your net worth.

Have you ever heard the term net worth? Do you really understand what it means? If not, you really need to understand it. It summarizes all of your finances into one simple number and really tells you where your personal finances stand.

I know it sounds like a horrible financial buzz word, but it is extremely valuable to understand. The first thing that comes to mind for most people when they hear net worth is some billionaire like Warren Buffet or Donald Trump. It's not just for billionaires!

By now you're probably like, what is it? Ok, ok, now that I've stressed the importance, here is what it is. Basically it is a simple formula:

- Total Assets - Total Debts = Net Worth

Here is a simple example to help you understand the whole picture of what we are doing:

Assets:

House - $100,000

Car - $10,000

Bank Account - $1,000

Investments - $9,000

Total Assets = $120,000

Debts:

Mortgage - $94,000

Car Loan - $5,000

Credit Card - $1,000

Total Debt = $100,000

Net Worth:

Total Assets ($120,000) - Total Debts ($100,000) = Net Worth ($20,000)

The bottom line is that this is how much money you are actually in possession of. It's your total financial picture in one number. If you thought of your money as a game, then your Net Worth is your score.

Calculate your own Net Worth in your Money Snapshot by taking your Total Assets and subtracting your Total Debt.

Add a final line, "Net Worth" to your Money Snapshot at the bottom.

How Can I Use My Net Worth?

You may be wondering how is this that helpful? Well, here is how you can use this number to your advantage. Each time you consider a major financial transaction think to yourself how it will affect your net worth. You want to ALWAYS be focused on increasing your net worth and making financial decisions that support that.

For example, taking more debt like credit card debt decreases the value of your net worth. That's not what you want to do if you want to be financially successful. Increasing the value of your assets like your house, your investments, or your bank account, increases your net worth, which is good!

Most all positive financial decisions and transactions increase your net worth and build your wealth. This makes it a great indicator of your financial health and where it is going. This is your financial score in life. Wealthy people are always focused on increasing their net worth each month and year. You have to focus on the same thing.

How To Maintain Your Money Snapshot

You have a completed Money Snapshot now! Your money is organized and you can quickly glance at it and see your entire financial picture. The problem is that your Money Snapshot shows your financial picture at a certain point in time. You have to keep it up.

Secret #5 - Money Snapshot

I recommend carving out one day per month to update your Money Snapshot. Put it on your calendar and do it that day every month. I personally like to review and update my Money Snapshot on the 1st of the month, every month.

Duplicate your current Money Snapshot and simply update it for the new month. You'll be able to see trends over the months, like your debt decreasing and your assets increasing which will begin to raise your net worth. It becomes a goal you can work towards each month to slowly increase your financial picture for the better.

There are also great online tools that you can use to connect your accounts to and it will automatically build your Money Snapshot for you. I'll talk more about that in the Money Automation Blueprint secret.

Now go take action and create your own Money Snapshot!

Action Steps

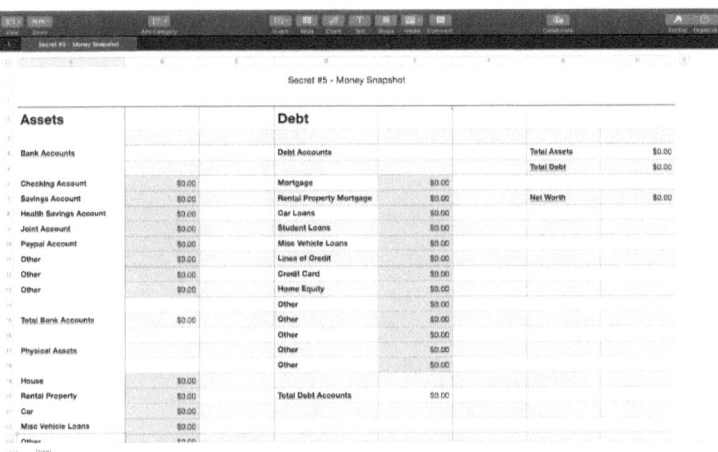

You'll find a spreadsheet that will make it even easier on the bonus materials site! It's time to make this happen:

- List out all of your bank accounts

- List out all of your physical assets

- List out all of your investments

- List out all of your debt

- Calculate your net worth

Secret #5 - Money Snapshot

- Create a Money Snapshot habit and update it monthly

Secret #6 - Perfect Budget

Some people hear the word budget and cringe. It's not that bad! In fact, it's pretty cool once you are done and able to see where all your money is coming from and where it is going. It gives you a really good sense of clarity and control over your financial picture. You need one. It's the #1 way you can get your money under control, start to eliminate debt, and begin building wealth.

I'm going to walk you through creating a simple and AWESOME budget just using paper and pen or a spreadsheet. Let's get started!

How This Budget Is Going To Work

First off, let's briefly talk about what we are going to do and how it works. This will be a "zero based budget." In normal words, this just means that every dollar you receive as income will be assigned to a budget category. There will be no income not budgeted.

To make it even simpler, imagine the old days. You get your paycheck and take it down to the bank and cash it. So now you've got a wad of real cash. Now, you take it home and sit down at the dining room table. You pull out a pack of envelopes and mark down all the various things you want to do with that money. Expenses like electricity and possibly savings for a vacation for example.

You stuff that cash in all the various envelopes. You do this until all the cash is gone. This is zero based budgeting. It's basically assigning every dollar to an expense. Eventually you'll need to pay the electricity bill or book that vacation and then you'll pull money out of that envelope and pay for it.

Make sense? That's basically what we are going to do, but with a modern twist. Get out a pencil and paper or open a spreadsheet and let's get started.

Add Your Income To Your Perfect Budget

The first thing you need to add is your income. Lucky for you, you already did the hard work in the Money Discovery of pulling all this information together.

Add "Monthly Income" at the top of the page.

Now, begin by adding all your income sources to the Monthly Income section. Make sure you look at your Money Discovery research. List out the amount you receive monthly from these sources as well.

Finally, let's add all your income sources together to create a "Total Monthly Income" Add up all of your monthly income to get a sum.

Add Your Monthly Bills To Your Perfect Budget

Next, we're going to add all your bills to the bills section. This info should also be already in your Money Discovery you completed earlier.

Add "Monthly Bills" at the top of the page in a new column.

Bills are simply anything you are billed for every month like electricity, Netflix, your phone bill, etc. Add in all your bills under the bills category. Put in the name of every bill and the amount. If it varies, I would estimate a bit high to make sure you have enough set aside. Once you've got all your bills listed, it's time to total it all up. Just like when totaled up your income, we'll do the same with all your bills.

Total them all up and put it in the field, "Total Monthly Bills"

Add Your Monthly Expenses To Your Perfect Budget

Now we're adding all your monthly expenses. Expenses are similar to bills, but these are things that you buy on your own rather than getting a bill for. A good example is fuel or groceries and luckily you've already pulled all your expenses together in your Money Discovery as well.

Add "Monthly Expenses" below your "Monthly Bills" section.

Add every expense you have and the monthly amount. It's most likely going to vary from month to month, but you'll have to come up with a good estimate. It's best to estimate high so that you are prepared for the worst case scenario in which you spend more than average on that expense for the month.

Total all of your expenses and in the field, "Total Monthly Expenses."

Add Your Financial Goals to Your Perfect Budget

Time to add your financial goals to your Perfect Budget. You've already thought up your financial goals in the Money Discovery and even broke them down into actionable monthly savings amounts. Take those goals and turn them into actions that can help you budget to get there in the future.

Add "Financial Goals" below your "Monthly Expenses" section.

Under the Financial Goals section list out everything you wanted to begin saving for and how much you need to save per month.

Add a final line called, "Total Financial Goals."

Finally, add up the total amount you'll need to save for your monthly goals and put that next to "Total Financial Goals."

How Much Do You Have Left To Budget?

You've made it to the final step! Let's figure out how much money you have left to budget!

Create a new line at the bottom of your Perfect Budget that says, "Money Left To Budget."

You'll need to use a formula to determine how much of our your income is left to budget if any. Basically what the formula will do is determine how much of your Total Monthly Income is left after subtracting the Total Monthly Bills, Total Monthly Expenses, and Total Financial Goals.

Here is the formula:

Money Left To Budget = Total Monthly Income - Total Monthly Bills - Total Monthly Expenses - Total Financial Goals

Boom! You have a final number. Now that number is either going to be positive or negative. If it's positive, you've got more money to budget. If all your expenses are covered you could add more to your goals like saving for financial freedom. If it's negative, you're spending more money than you have coming in. It's time to make some changes. Can you eliminate some of those expenses? If not, you may have to lower your expectations for your goals.

In the Bills Conquerer secret I'll show you how to decrease your bills and expenses. Either way, you want to get Money Left To Budget back to $0. Make any adjustments necessary to get it back to $0.

What About Monthly Transactions?

You may be wondering what about a section for transactions? Every time you buy something you may want to know how much you have left in each expense category or goals.

Yes, it's totally possible to create another tab in your worksheet or paper to track your transactions and calculate all that up for your based on your transactions but let's not do that. Why?

A spreadsheet or paper is not the best tool for doing that. There are way better tools to do that and in the Money Automation Blueprint secret I'll dig into how to use a tool do just that in a much better and efficient way.

What the spreadsheet budget is great for is, understanding your money and getting a grasp on where it's going, but it should only be a starting point and we'll expand on how to use your Perfect Budget monthly in the Money Automation Blueprint secret.

Here Is A Simple Example Perfect Budget

Monthly Income

Paycheck: $2,000

Total Monthly Income: $2,000

Monthly Bills

Rent: $600

Electricity: $150

Phone: $75

Water: $50

Internet: $75

Credit Card $250

Insurance: $50

Total Monthly Bills: $1,250

Monthly Expenses

Groceries: $400

Gas: $50

Eating Out: $100

Total Expenses: $550

<u>Financial Goals</u>

Wedding: $200

<u>Money Left To Budget</u>

Money Left To Budget: $0

Control And Understanding Of Your Money

After putting this together I'm hoping you're having an "AH HA" moment about your money. This is what the Perfect Budget is for. It guides your plan and strategy for your money.

Secret #6 - Perfect Budget

You will need to review your transactions each week to make sure you are sticking to your budget and update your budget monthly for any changes that are needed.

Look for the Money Automation Blueprint secret later in the book, where I'll take your Perfect Budget to the next level with automatic transaction importing and categorization to make sure your money is following your Perfect Budget.

Action Steps

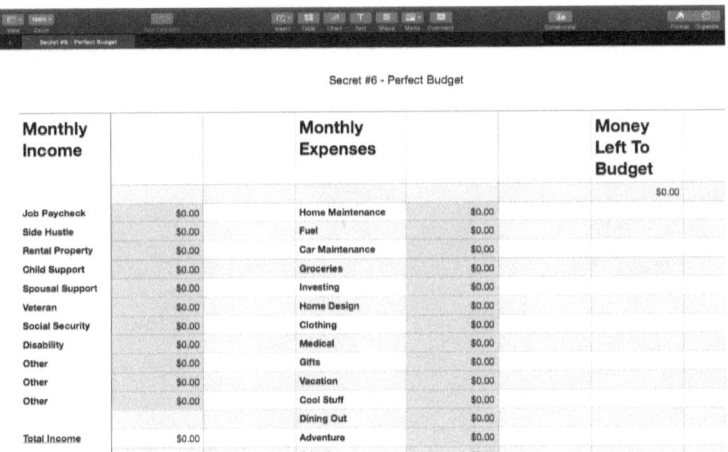

You'll find a spreadsheet that will make it even easier on the bonus materials site! Now it's time to make this happen:

- Add your monthly income
- Add your monthly bills
- Add your monthly expenses
- Add your financial goals

-     Calculate your money left to budget

Secret #7 - Bills Conqueror

Bills are like little leaches. They latch onto your bank account and start sucking the money out slowly. Sometimes, not enough for you to even notice the damage they are doing to you. I'm going to help you break off those leaches and get your bills under control. Not only will this give you more money to save and invest so you can reach financial freedom faster, but it will also help to relieve the stress that bills can have on you.

There's nothing like the stress of paying your bills and not having enough money to pay them or the stress and overwhelm of dealing with all the different due dates and websites to pay them. You're going to break that cycle for good.

Secret #7 - Bills Conqueror

I've been guilty of allowing bills to build up and drain my checking account in the past too. Initially I started out with a few bills, but it begins to add up fast. First, I needed a cell phone plan, then suddenly I felt the need for Netflix, and then I'm adding Spotify... It goes on and on.

Businesses have learned the power of recurring payments. Have you noticed how everything is sold in monthly plans now rather than one time payments? It's an easy way for businesses to continue sucking your money out of your bank account each month.

Recurring payments are also deceiving because they make an expensive product seem inexpensive. For example, you may think that Netflix is a super deal at $13.99 per month. At first glance yeah that's awesome for what they're giving you, but when you look at the real cost it is much higher.

That Netflix plan is actually costing you $168 per year and imagine if you stick with Netflix for multiple years. That $168 is actually $840 over 5 years. It's not as cheap as it seems and this is just one example. Look at your phone plan. Let's just say it's $60 per month. That little bill is $720 a year and $3,600 over 5 years.

When you add in all of your bills it really adds up and consumes so much of your relatively small salary that a typical 9 - 5 job is willing to pay you. Even with a college degree.

So, even the smallest decrease in your bills can make a huge impact on your money. The more money you can save from the bill leaches, the more money you can save and invest to reach financial freedom so much faster.

I'll show you another example that really drives home the process of conquering your bills.

Imagine Your Checking Account Is A Bucket

Yep, you read that right. Imagine your checking account is a bucket. Imagine it is hanging from a rope by the handle. I'll take a hose and start spraying water into it at a small trickle rate. What happens? That bucket or (checking account) begins to fill up slowly. That water from the hose is your income and money. The hose is the company you work for.

So, this is great initially, your bucket is filling up slowly and you're happy. Eventually, it'll get so full you need to add buckets for savings and investing, but that's in the future.

Now here I come with a drill. I've got lots of different sized drill bits. So, you decide you want to get Netflix. No problem, I'll take a small drill bit less than the size of a pencil and drill a hole in your bucket from the bottom.

Now, you've got a trickle of water coming out of your bucket. That hole is Netflix slowly draining just a little bit of water out of your bucket. Your inflow from the house is much bigger than the hole so your bucket is still filling but a little bit slower.

Now, maybe you decide you want an unlimited phone plan with some extra features. I'll take a marble sized drill bit and drill another hole. Now you've got water coming out faster.

As you continue adding bills the water drains faster making it harder and harder to pour enough water from the house to keep it from draining.

What usually happens is people take on bills until they can't keep the water from immediately draining. You'll never get ahead this way. You'll never have extra water for more buckets. You're basically working to give companies your water (or money, hypothetically).

What you need to do now is start plugging those holes so you can begin to fill your bucket. I'll show you how.

Let's Review Your Bills

This is where the Money Discovery will help you again. Go back to your Money Discovery and pull out your bills list. Grab a paper and pencil or open up a spreadsheet and let's get busy. List out all your bills from your Money Discovery.

For each bill I want you to review the bill and categorize into it 1 of 3 categories. Here are the categories:

Need

These are bills that you absolutely need for basic living. Some examples are:

- Shelter (Home or Apartment)
- Electricity

- Water

For each bill that is a need write Need next to it.

Want

These are bills that you want, but don't need. Some examples are:

- Netflix
- Spotify
- Cable TV

For each bill that is a want write Want next to it.

Don't Need Or Want

Any bills that are left are categorized as Don't Need or Want. Go ahead and write that next to the remaining bills or simply put an X next them.

These are usually bills that you signed up for in the past but no longer need or just simply forgot they were still billing you.

Clean Up Your Bills

Now let's start saving some money!

Cancel The Don't Need Or Want Bills

The first thing you will want to do is cancel those bills that you don't need and you don't want. These are the holes in your bucket that you need to plug. These are the easy wins right off the bat.

Review Your Wants

Now look at your wants. Are they really worth the cost? Let's say you have a subscription to Netflix, Hulu, and HBO. Do you really need all 3? Often having more isn't better, it begins to become overwhelming.

You also have to factor in what you want more. Do you want to reach financial freedom faster or watch Hulu occasionally? It's ok if you really enjoy it. If the subscription creates absolute joy in your life, keep it. That's what money is for. A tool to enjoy your life. Don't make yourself miserable, but look for bills that are not adding enough value in your life to keep.

If there are any Want bills that you decided you don't need, go ahead and cancel those as well.

Minimize Those Bills

For the remaining bills, you will need to try to lower those bills. Not all bills can be lowered, but you'd probably be surprise how many bills you can get lowered. There are couple ways you can do that.

Price Comparison

This is an easy way to lower your bills. Let's say you have a phone plan for $80 per month. Compare 2 other phone providers in your area and compare their prices. Often you will find that you can find a cheaper plan at another company. Prices creep up and often other companies may offer you discount bonuses to sign up for their service instead.

Do this for each of your bills and I guarantee you, you will find savings.

Negotiation

If you can't find a better price from another provider, negotiation is the next tactic. For your remaining bills, call the company and tell them that you can't justify the price of their service anymore and are considering cancelling their service. Ask them if they can offer you a better rate before cancelling.

This doesn't work every time, but it works enough to make it worth your time and possibly save you a lot of money in the long run. Remember, that even small decreases in your monthly bill price can add up to huge savings over the next year.

Next Step

Once you've finished reviewing your bills, the next step will be to automate your bills. I'll show you how to automate them in the Money Automation Blueprint secret later. For now enjoy your wins and extra money!

Make sure to review your bills at least every 6 months to make sure no new and unwanted bills have popped up or that your current bills haven't increased too much.

Action Steps

You'll find a spreadsheet that will make it even easier on the bonus materials site! Now it's time to make this happen:

- List out all of your bills
- Sort your bills
  * Needs
  * Wants
  * Don't Need or Want
- Cancel unneeded bills
- Review your wants
- Price compare your remaining bills
- Negotiate the price of your remaining bills

Secret #8 - Debt Elimination Plan

I've been there. Thousands of dollars in debt, feeling trapped with no way out. But there is absolutely a way out!

I graduated college buried in debt. Between outrageous student loans, car loans, and credit cards I left our college system in over $80,000 dollars of debt. All this while raising my two wonderful children and living off a tiny little salary. What a great way to start your adult life! I was stressed, but you know what? I escaped it and if I can do it, you can too. It's really not that hard with the Debt Elimination Plan.

I'll not only show you how, but I'll also show you how to automate the process in the Money Automation Blueprint secret so you don't even have to worry about it!

In this secret, I'll cover creating your plan, but what makes this work so well is that I automated it so that I escaped debt without even thinking about it. Every month my debt got lower and lower but I wasn't doing hardly anything on my part, it was all automated! If you're looking to get out from the under the burden of debt keep reading, we're going to do it right now.

You're already aware of this, but debt is bad! So bad it can affect your health if you're constantly thinking about it and worrying about it. You can stop all of that and erase it from your mind. Wouldn't it be great to not even have to think about debt? It's 100% possible. So how do you do it?

The basic idea is to pay off your debt from smallest to largest debt. Pay the minimum payment to all debts but the smallest one. The goal is to eliminate them one by one by focusing on one at a time. Each time you pay off a debt you gain confidence and momentum to knock out the next one. This strategy works. This is the basis for what I used to escape debt but I took it the next level and created my own strategy I called the Debt Elimination Plan.

Stop Feeding The Debt

Stop using debt! This is probably the hardest step in the whole process. You have to stop increasing your debt, today! Some people can put away their credit cards and leave them and for others it's not so easy. They see a new gadget and they just have to have it. They pull out their credit card and continue the downward spiral into the debt hole. If you are one of those people don't feel bad. It's human nature and you can overcome it.

Cut up all of your credit cards now! Literally cut them up and throw them in the trash. If you have any other access to debt like a Line of Credit or paper checks for your credit cards, cut them up and throw them away also. Just by stopping your access to debt you've accomplished a huge step. Pat yourself on the back, because you are officially on the road to being debt free!

Identify All Your Debt

Just thinking about all the debt is probably stressing you out alone. The whole purpose of the Debt Elimination Plan is to get rid of that stress. This is the first step to eliminating it.

We are going to list out all of your debt. It is necessary to know exactly what you owe to solve the problem. So get busy and list all of your debt. Luckily for you, you did a lot that research already in the Money Discovery.

Once you are finished listing all your debt you will already begin to feel satisfaction that you are taking the necessary steps to conquer you debt and eliminate that stress from your life for good!

Determine How Much You Can Pay Towards Your Debt

You must decide exactly how much you are going to put aside each month to eliminate that debt. Take a look at your income and expenses from your Perfect Budget to figure out what you can spend each month to get rid of that debt.

Choose how much you want to set aside of your Perfect Budget to put towards debt. Put as much as you can, but don't squeeze yourself so much that you have nothing left for other needs. That will only demoralize you and ultimately make you more likely to fall out of the plan.

Once you've found how much you can apply to your debt payments, let's find the best way to apply that money to your debt and eliminate it!

Create Your Debt Elimination Plan

Now we are going to create your plan to get out of debt. This is where your list of debts you created earlier comes in handy. Pull up that list and take a look at all of your debts. We are going to create a new list from those debts.

Start by listing the debt with the lowest balance. Now, list the next debt with the next lowest balance. Continue doing this for all of your debts until you have all of your debts sorted from lowest to highest balance.

The first one, which is the one with the lowest balance, will be the debt you focus on from now on until it is paid off. I call it the Focus Debt.

In the previous step you determined how much money you can put towards the debt. Now let's make a plan on how to use that money to pay off your debt in the best way possible.

Secret #8 - Debt Elimination Plan

Using this simple formula we'll find out how much of that money should be paid to the Focus Debt by subtracting the minimum payments of each debt other than your Focus Debt from your debt repayment money:

Debt Repayment Money - Debt 2 Minimum Payment - Debt 3 Minimum Payment - (Continue For Each Debt) = Focus Debt Payment

Here is an example:

$1,000 (Debt Repayment Money) - $120 (Debt 2 Minimum Payment) - $160 (Debt 3 Minimum Payment) = $720 Towards Focus Debt

Now list out your debt plan like the following example:

- Focus Debt - $720 Monthly Payment
- Debt 2 - $120 Monthly Payment
- Debt 3 - $160 Monthly Payment

At this point your stress will be melting away even more! Not only do you know exactly how much debt you have and where it all is. You have a plan to eliminate it!

Once you are finished creating your plan you will already begin to feel satisfaction that you are taking the necessary steps to conquer you debt and eliminate that stress from your life for good!

Lowering Your Interest Rate

While paying down your focus debt, it is possible, if you have a good credit score, to get a debt consolidation loan. Payoff and Lending Tree are a couple of examples of companies that can loan you money at a lower interest rate to payoff your existing debt and then you pay the debt consolidation company instead at a better rate.

This works if you have good credit. If you do, then it is highly recommended do a debt consolidation load to reduce the amount of money going to interest.

If you have a 700 or above credit score you'll likely get a better rate. Apply for a debt consolidation loan and compare the offer rate to your existing debt. If it is lower and there are no significant fees to pay, then debt consolidation makes sense for you.

Next Steps

So at this point, you know how much you owe and all the details. You have a plan and know how much you need to pay each lender.

Now, it's time to put the rubber to the road and take action. In the Money Automation Blueprint secret, I'll show you how to automate your debt elimination plan so it takes care of the debt for you while you focus on what you love. Make sure to review your Debt Elimination Plan monthly to update it as debts are paid off or circumstances have changed.

If you've followed the steps, you now have a Debt Elimination Plan. You're on your way to debt freedom, you have peace of mind, and you can focus on what's important to you! You've made a huge step forward in your financial well being!

Action Steps

Debts	Balance	->	Prioritized Debts	Balance	Minimum Payment	
Car Loans	$0.00			$0.00	$0.00	<- Focus Debt
Student Loans	$0.00			$0.00	$0.00	
Misc Vehicle Loans	$0.00			$0.00	$0.00	
Lines of Credit	$0.00			$0.00	$0.00	
Credit Card	$0.00			$0.00	$0.00	
Home Equity	$0.00			$0.00	$0.00	
Other	$0.00			$0.00	$0.00	
Other	$0.00			$0.00	$0.00	
Other	$0.00			$0.00	$0.00	
Other	$0.00			$0.00	$0.00	
Other	$0.00			$0.00	$0.00	
How Much I Can Pay Monthly	$0.00		Focus Debt Payment	$0.00		

Secret #8 - Debt Elimination Plan

Secret #8 - Debt Elimination Plan

You'll find a spreadsheet that will make it even easier on the bonus materials site! Now it's time to make this happen:

- Stop using debt
- Eliminate your access to debt
- List out all of your debts
- Determine how much you can pay toward your debts
- Sort your debts from lowest to largest balance
- Determine how much to pay towards each debt
- Begin paying down your debt
- Consolidate your debt if the debt consolidation loan is a better rate

Section Three: Wealth

These are probably the most exciting secrets of the book for most people and YES this is my favorite part of the book. However, if you haven't implemented the secrets in part one and two, you're never going to get ahead with your money, no matter how great these upcoming secrets are. Do yourself a huge favor and go back and finish section one and two before starting this section. If you've already done that, ignore my rant, let's rock this!

In this section you are going to learn how to save money, how much to save, and how long it will take you to reach financial freedom in Secret #9 - Savings Roadmap.

You're going to learn how to invest that money and turn it into more money than you ever thought possible in Secret #10 - Ultimate Investing Strategy.

I'll show you the secrets of the wealthy and how to make more money at your 9-5 in Secret #11 - Income Amplifier!

Finally, we'll wrap everything up as I show you the secret to automate everything you've learned in this book in Secret #12 - Money Automation Blueprint.

I'm so excited to share these secrets with you and change your life forever. Let's get started with Secret #9.

Secret #9 - Savings Roadmap

The average amount of money Americans save per year is about 3% of their income… 3%! That's a horrible amount of savings. In other words, Americans spend about 97% of the money they make! It comes into their bank account and 97% is pretty much gone. Vanished into thin air. Actually, it goes to paying bills, buying food, buying things, etc, but, we can do way better than that.

Building Wealth Starts Here

This is where wealth building begins. Remember, it's not what you make, it's how much you keep. You are most likely never going to build any wealth if you don't save money. If you don't pay yourself first. If you want financial security, you have to save.

The next time your car breaks down, how are you going to pay for it? Reach for a credit card? That only makes matters worse. Now, what if you had $1,000 sitting in the bank account ready for your emergency? Not only is that better financially, but the peace of mind it gives you is priceless!

Saving money is a huge step forward. Once you begin to save money, you begin to build freedom. Each dollar saved brings you one step closer to financial freedom. Don't think of saving money as losing spendable money. Think of it as investing in yourself. It's one of the best financial steps you can take.

I'm going to break down the Savings Roadmap to help you get on track for long-term financial wealth and eventually financial freedom.

The Emergency Fund

The very first thing you need to do is build an Emergency Fund. It's nearly impossible to stop living paycheck to paycheck when you have no funds available for day to day unexpected events.

Let's say your car breaks down. Your furnace stops working. How are you going to pay for it? Most people grab their credit card. That's not the best way to handle it. Once you put it in on your credit card, you're paying interest on the balance. You're still on the hook for new day to day unexpected expenses while paying down a credit card as well.

It can be a downward spiral that's hard to get out of. You go into debt and struggle even more. This is the way of the paycheck to paycheck lifestyle.

The first step to building wealth is to begin an Emergency Fund. If you have one, then skip forward. If not, let's create one now.

You need the funds fast at times so it's best to have it out of your checking account, but easily available. I suggest opening another account at your bank like a savings account if you don't have one yet.

The $100 Fund

Let's start small. For the next month transfer $25 per week into your Emergency Fund account. If you don't have enough, look at your Perfect Budget and see what you can exclude to get the money. Could you sell some junk at your house or do some work on the side?

At the end of the month, you will have $100 saved for emergencies.

The $500 Fund

$100 won't cover too much in today's prices, so do a little celebration and then let's get back to work. Now let's crank it up a notch. Review your expenses and see how you can save $50 per week. Can you stop going out to eat once a week? Sell some old stuff in the house?

After 2 months you will have $500. Now this is more significant. Yeah, it won't cover huge expenses, but now you have a little breathing room. Now you can cover some small emergencies on you car or house. Do a little celebration and then move onto the next challenge.

The $1,000 Fund

The final step is to get to $1,000. This covers a lot of day to day unexpected expenses. This will give you the breathing room to be able to handle that expense without grabbing a credit card and stressing out over the issue.

You have a couple choices:

- Continue adding $50 per week to your fund. It will take you about 2 1/2 months to reach $1,000.
- Contribute $125 per week and reach your goal within 1 month.

Either way, you hit your goal. Do whatever you can afford. This is only the beginning. Once you've reached $1,000 you have new goals to work towards. Try to work towards contributing 5% of your income going forward to your Emergency Fund.

Continue building that habit and shoot for these goals in the future:

- 1 Month of Living Expenses
- 3 Months of Living Expenses
- 6 Months of Living Expenses
- 9 Months of Living Expenses
- 1 Year of Living Expenses

As you build up your Emergency Fund you build up your freedom. You are no longer dependent on a job to pay for emergencies. You are no longer struggling by living paycheck to paycheck. The Emergency Fund is your first step to building wealth and financial freedom.

In the next secret I'll show how to invest any money in your Emergency Fund over $1,000 and grow it so much faster.

The $1k Roadmap

Here's a breakdown of the above plan you can follow easily each week as you go:

- Week 1 - $25 - Total: $25
- Week 2 - $25 - Total: $50
- Week 3 - $25 - Total: $75
- Week 4 - $25 - Total: $100
- Week 5 - $50 - Total: $150
- Week 6 - $50 - Total: $200
- Week 7 - $50 - Total: $250
- Week 8 - $50 - Total: $300
- Week 9 - $50 - Total: $350
- Week 10 - $50 - Total: $400
- Week 11 - $50 - Total: $450
- Week 12 - $50 - Total: $500
- Week 13 - $50 - Total: $550
- Week 14 - $50 - Total: $600
- Week 15 - $50 - Total: $650

- Week 16 - $50 - Total: $700
- Week 17 - $50 - Total: $750
- Week 18 - $50 - Total: $800
- Week 19 - $50 - Total: $850
- Week 20 - $50 - Total: $900
- Week 21 - $50 - Total: $950
- Week 22 - $50 - Total: $1,000

How To Increase Your Savings

It feels like there is never enough money and never a good enough time to save money, but there is always a way. I'm going to show you a couple strategies that can help you save and with some of them, you will never even notice the money is missing!

Saving Your Raises and Bonuses

For most people, when we get a raise or a bonus, we go out, celebrate, and come up with all kinds of ideas about how to spend that money, but that's not exactly the best idea. Now, don't get me wrong. It's ok to spend some of that money, but you're better off putting most, if not all of that money towards savings.

Bare minimum, put at least 50% towards savings. The fact is, you'll probably never even miss the money because you didn't have it before. As soon as you get a raise or bonus set aside that money or at least a portion of it. Also, if it's a raise, schedule an automatic transfer to savings so you don't even have to think about it, which leads us to strategy #2.

Automating Your Savings

If you have any type of modern bank they probably have an automatic transfer feature. This simply allows you to setup a transfer to a savings account on a set schedule. For example, you could set up your bank account to automatically transfer money each day to a savings account.

The more you can set aside the better. Automatic transfers take care of doing it for you, so you don't have to worry about it. Automatic is the key. Automate your money. You don't have to worry about forgetting or stressing about the money, it's simply moved out and you probably won't even notice or miss it.

In the Money Automation Blueprint secret, I'll show you more about how to automate your savings so you don't think about and won't even miss it, but for now at least setup an automated transfer to separate bank account like a savings account.

Action Steps

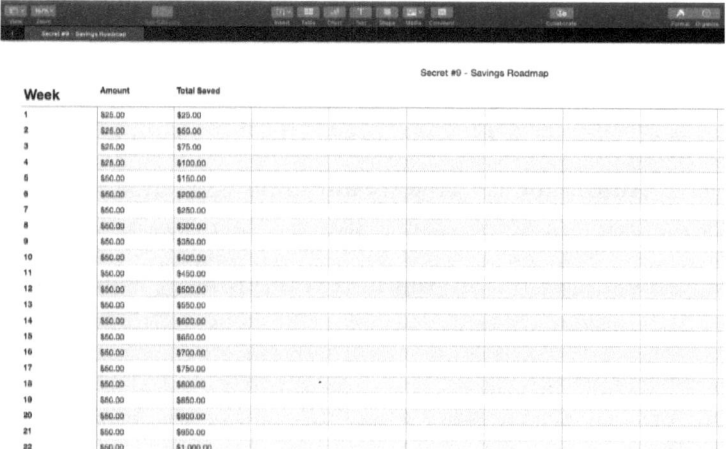

You'll find a spreadsheet that will make it even easier on the bonus materials site! Now it's time to make this happen:

- Commit to saving some money

- Begin building your Emergency Fund

- Save at least a portion if not all of your next bonus or raise.

- Create an automatic transfer in your bank account.

Secret #10 - Ultimate Investing Strategy

This is one of my favorite secrets in the book. I've been investing since I was in college and love it. I've made more money investing than I ever thought I would and it just keeps on growing.

After I graduated high school, I was on an adult kick and was trying to be more responsible. I headed down to my local bank with $500 and opened up my first certificate of deposit (CD). For the next 6 months, my CD gained about 2% interest… That's terrible.

Today it is so much easier to save money and even invest it for much better returns and I'm going to show you how. Once you've begun to build your Emergency Fund and are contributing to it, you need to begin investing. I'm going to show you all the accounts you should be investing with.

The 401k

The 401k is a great investment opportunity if you have access to one. If you work for a company they likely already have one available to you. If you aren't already enrolled in your companies 401k, you need to do it ASAP. You're leaving money on the table each day you don't have a 401k. Talk to your HR contact at your company and get enrolled right away. I'll tell you why you should be investing in your 401k.

Types Of 401k's

There are two common 401k's that your company may offer you. Here is a simple breakdown of the differences:

401k

In a regular 401k, you don't pay taxes on the money you are contributing to your 401k. The downside is that when you do withdraw from your 401k you will have to pay taxes on those 401k funds as income.

Roth 401k

In a Roth 401k, you pay taxes on the money you contribute to your Roth 401k.

The plus side is that when you withdraw money from your 401k you won't have to pay taxes on it. This is a pretty good plus.

Which 401k Is Right For You?

If I had to choose between the two, I would take the Roth 401k over the regular 401k. In most circumstances, your taxes will be higher when you withdraw from your 401k and your balance will be much bigger. I would rather pay taxes now rather than later on my 401K.

Company Match

One of the best features of a 401k is the awesome company match! Your company most likely will contribute a certain percentage of your salary to your 401k if you contribute. Every company is different but a common scenario is that your company will contribute 3% of your income to your 401K if you contribute 6%. That's a total of 9%! This is an awesome deal you shouldn't be passing up on. If you're not getting your company match, sign up now! Check with your HR reps to verify you are meeting the requirements for the match!

How To Invest In Your 401k

What to invest in is always up for debate, but my two favorite investing options are:

1 - Age Target Date Funds

This is a fund that invests based on when you expect to retire. You are basically handing the reigns of your investment options over to professionals. This is fine if you want a totally hands off, give it to someone else, approach.

The one thing to watch for is the fees. Fee's will eat up your returns over time. Look for the lowest fee possible. The best fees are ideally less than 1% if possible.

2 - S&P 500 Index ETF's

These are my personal favorite for a 401K. The great thing about these funds is that they generally have very low fees. Sometimes the fees are less than .10%.

These funds also include stocks from the 500 biggest companies in the stock market. It's a diversified mix of stocks that track the entire stock market. Over history, the S&P 500 Index has averaged around 11% returns. That's not bad returns at all.

How Much Should You Invest?

My goal is to always invest at least 10% of my income into my 401k. Always make sure you are getting your company match. If you have to invest more than 10% to get that match then do it. It's free money!

At this point, you should be contributing 5% of your income to your Emergency Fund and 10% to your 401k. Now we'll talk about another great fund you should be investing in.

The IRA

The IRA is similar to a 401K but you can open one without working for an employer. If you are self-employed the IRA is a great alternative to the 401k.

If you have a 401k already, the IRA is a great addition for retirement savings. You can sign up for an IRA with apps that make it super easy. I'll show you more about that in Money Automation Blueprint secret.

IRA Vs Roth IRA

Again, there are two common types of IRA's you can choose from. Here is a simple breakdown of the differences:

IRA

Just like the 401k's, a regular IRA allows you to contribute to the IRA tax-free.

The downside again is that you will pay taxes on it later when you withdraw on a higher balance and most likely higher tax bracket.

ROTH IRA

A Roth IRA contributions are added on already taxed money. The upside is that you can withdrawal tax-free in the future.

Which IRA Is Right For You?

If I had to choose between the two, I would take the Roth IRA just like I would take the Roth 401k. In most circumstances, your taxes will be higher when you withdraw from your IRA and your balance will be much bigger. I would rather pay taxes now rather than later on my Roth IRA so the growth can be withdrawn tax-free.

How To Invest In Your IRA

What to invest in is always up for debate, but my two favorite investing options are the same as the 401k options:

1 - Age Target Date Funds

This is a fund that invests its portfolio based on when you expect to retire. You are basically handing the reigns of your investment options over to professionals.

This is fine if you want a totally hands off, give it to someone else, approach. The one thing to watch for is the fees. Fee's will eat up your returns over time. Look for the lowest fee possible. The best fees are ideally less than 1% if possible.

2 - S&P 500 Index ETF's

These are my personal favorite for a Roth IRA. The great thing about these funds is that they generally have very low fees. Sometimes the fees are less than .10%.

These funds also include stocks from the 500 biggest companies in the stock market. It's a diversified mix of stocks that track the entire stock market. Over history, the S&P 500 Index has averaged around 11% returns. That's not bad returns at all.

How Much Should You Invest?

If you already have a 401k and are investing at least 10% into it, it's best to contribute at least 5% of your income to your IRA. If you don't have a 401k and don't have access to one then it's best to contribute at least 15% to your IRA. At this point you should be contributing at least 5% to your Emergency Fund, 10% to your 401k and 5% to your IRA.

Stock Investing

Before we start talking about investing in stocks. Let's make sure you have the essentials completed FIRST:

- Investing 5% in your Emergency Fund
- Investing 10% in your 401k and obtaining your company match
- Investing 5% in your IRA or 15% if you don't can't open a 401k

Once you've saved $1,000 in your Emergency Fund, continue to save that 5%, but instead of placing the money in your savings account, begin contributing it to your stock investing account. If you can save more than 20% of your income as suggested above, save any additional amount to your stock investing account as well. I'm going to show you in this secret how to invest in stocks and make great gains on those investments.

The Money Tree

I've made over $100,000 in the stock market. Have I told you that I love investing in stocks? Well, I do. It's one of the best ways to take your money and turn it into more money!

Recently I was talking to my wife about our stocks. I looked over and saw our little money tree chilling on a table and I said, that's what our stocks are like. They're like a money tree that keeps on giving! But, just like all of life, it's not that simple. You can't just jump into stocks and begin making money without any understanding of what you're doing.

To make money in stocks you have to:

- Have some money to invest with
- Understand how to pick stocks that will actually make money

According to Market Watch, about 1 in 20 mutual fund managers beat the S&P 500. (The S&P 500 is the biggest 500 companies in the stock market & this is why we stick to S&P 500 Index funds in our 401k and IRA's)

If only 1 out 20 stock pros can actually make more money than just following the biggest 500 companies how the heck are you going to do it? I've done it every year since

I've begun investing and I'm going to show you my favorite strategy to do it.

My Stock Investing Strategy Is Long Term

One thing you have to know up front is that my strategy is long term. I'm not doing any day trading or quick buy and sells with this strategy. I buy and hold for extended periods of times.

The great thing about doing it this way is that it makes it easier for anyone to get into stock trading. Even if you have a day job and work while the stock exchange is open, no problem. You won't be staring at stock charts all day so it won't interfere with your daily life.

With this strategy, I am creating a money tree and watching it grow. It's long-term, so I only take money out if it is absolutely needed. If your looking for a day trading strategy look elsewhere because this definitely is not it. If you're still on board, let's rock. Here is my Ultimate Stock Investing Strategy:

1 - Open An Investing Account

Before you can even begin to start investing, you'll need to open an account. I love Robinhood. It's one of the best investing apps out there. It has a great web and app interface. It has $0 fees. Yes, you read that right! No fees at all. It's super easy to use and they just keep building onto it.

Open an account at www.robinhood.com and add your bank account. Transfer your starting funds and in a day or two you'll have your money in your account and you'll be ready to get started!

2 - Invest Enough Money To Make Good Returns Fast

Yes, you can start investing today with $100 dollars or less, but if you want to make money in stocks, especially, big money. You're going to need to invest some serious money to get it rolling.

Now, I would never suggest you start investing today with $10,000 when you are still learning how to invest in stocks, but if you want to start making some serious, life-changing money in stocks, you're going to have to go full fledge in.

$10,000 is a good starting point to begin making some serious money in stocks. If you're brand new, start small. Play with $100 to $500, but continue saving your money to get a much higher balance once you have a handle on what you are doing.

With $10,000 you can easily make an average jobs pay for the day if the markets are doing well you know how to invest! Plus some of my favorite stocks are over $1,000 per share, so you can't even get access to them when you have $500 to work with.

So, start small to learn, but also continue saving some money to really boost your investment account quickly.

3 - Brainstorm Your Dream Team of Companies / Stocks

It's time to brainstorm! Grab a piece of paper and pen or open up your laptop. Now we are going to create a list of potential stocks to invest in.

Have you ever seen fantasy football? I like to think of stock picking kind of like fantasy football. A group football fans get together and draft a team of their favorite players. The ones they think are going to take them to the super bowl.

I think of my stock portfolio the same way. I try to pull together a list of the best stocks that I think are going to bring me huge profits. So sit down and start thinking about your dream team. List out as many stocks as you can think of that you may want on your dream team.

Think of brands you absolutely love! You swear by them. These are potential candidates. Think of companies that you just know are going to take off over the next few years. Think about what you know. I've worked in the IT industry for a long time, so I've come to know tech. I have a knack for identifying tech companies that are really taking off.

What industry do you work in? Do you have knowledge of what the goto companies are in your industry? List out at least 10 companies or more if you'd like that you think would be great companies for your dream team.

4 - Diversify Your Stocks

Once you've got a list of stocks that you think will be star players and will bring in the cash, it's time to make sure you have a diversified set of stocks. There are 11 stock sectors. Ideally, your stocks will be spread across different sectors. Sectors just means the industries the companies are in.

Here are the stock sectors:

- Financial - Banks, Investments, Insurance
- Utilities - Electric, Water, Gas
- Consumer Products Discretionary - Products that we want but don't have to have

- Consumer Staples - Products that are hard to give up but not absolutely necessary
- Energy - Oil and Gas Companies
- Healthcare - Hospital, Pharmacy's, Doctors
- Industrials - Machinery, Building, Airplanes
- Technology - Software Companies, Electronics, IT
- Telecommunication - Wireless Providers, Cable, Internet
- Materials - Mining, Chemicals, Forestry
- Real Estate - Residential, Commercial, Retail

Can your stocks fit into several different categories? Try to make sure you have at least 5 different sectors covered if possible.

5 - Growth, Growth, Growth

So, how do we know these stocks you picked are going to go up? Do you know what makes stock prices rise? It's when more people are trying to buy a stock than trying to sell it. That makes the price rise.

Secret #10 - Ultimate Investing Strategy

So, what makes investors want to buy stocks in the first place? It's generally when the company is expected to grow faster than expected. Companies who are doing well make money. They make lots of money. The more money they make, the more they are growing.

Companies report to investors quarterly on how much they made for the quarter. Investors try to guess how much they will make. If the company exceeds that, boom! The stock usually soars.

So bottom line, you want to find companies that are growing like crazy and have the future potential to grow. Just like in real estate where they say the most important thing is location, location, location. In stocks, the most important thing is growth, growth, growth!

Review your companies to determine if each quarter their earnings are growing and beating investors expectations.

Basically, earnings are:

Income - Expenses = Earnings

It's also known as net income.

A solid company will have great earnings growth. So take a look at any financial site like finance.google.com and pull up one of the companies you were looking at and check the past 3 years of earnings. Have they gone up, down, or stagnated? If they are going up you may have a good stock. If earnings are going down or stagnating I would avoid them.

6 - Find Those Unique Companies That Dominate Their Market

Think about a type of business like coffee. Who is dominating? Who is so unique they don't have much competition. Here is an easy example, who dominates the coffee market? Starbucks of course. They have created a unique experience and dominate that market.

Who creates an amazing electric automobile that no one has been able to match? Tesla dominates the electric car market. These are examples of companies who have dominated their market or niche.

Look at the companies you picked earlier. Are they dominating the market or are they merely a competitor in a sea of the same old companies? If they are a market leader and don't have much competition in that area, you may have a winner. If they are just a same old, same old company then stay away.

7 - Find The Momentum

Momentum can be good or bad. It is a steady increase in the price of the stock over a period of time. The bad side of momentum is when everyone is jumping on a stock because the price is going higher, but there is no good data backing it up. At this point, it becomes a fools game of who is the greater fool. Eventually, you run out of fools and there isn't anyone left to buy and drive the price up and the stock crashes.

Obviously, we don't want to jump on bad momentum, but want we want to find is good momentum. Some stocks just stagnate even though they have solid fundamentals. When the public notices its potential and starts buying, it begins to rise. Now the price is moving upwards at a steady rate. This is the best place to buy in.

If you've found a company with all the previous criteria and has suddenly been increasing in price over a 3 month period that is a good sign of the potential continued increase in price.

The final key to momentum is knowing when to jump off momentum train. The best strategy is to continue to monitor the previous criteria and the upcoming fine print in the next section. If any of the key criteria you used to choose the stocks changes for the worse. That's a good indicator the momentum is coming to an end and it is time to sell the stock.

8 - Don't Ignore The Details

This section is a little technical but it's great to know this information. It's kind of like the vitals or health of the companies stock. So, to check this information you are going to need to pull up your favorite stock site like finance.google.com.

Revenue - This is the total amount of money the company has earned during the time frame you selected. Revenue should be rising over the past 3 years.

Earnings - This is the money the company actually kept during the time frame you selected. As I explained in #2 you want to find a company in which the earnings have been growing over at least the past 3 years.

Debt - Just like personal debt it can be bad and you don't want the company you buy to have too much. You'll see below how to determine how much is too much in the debt to asset ratio.

Equity - This is calculated by taking assets - liabilities. Equity is always good. You'll see how to measure the companies use of equity in the Return on Equity ratio below.

Price to Earnings Ratio (P/E) - This is basically the current stock price divided by the earnings per share. This gives you an idea of how much you are paying for the stock versus what they are actually earning. This gives you a comparison number versus other stocks and how expensive they are.

By itself, I would not put too much stock in it, but when comparing stocks to other stocks and using all the other data I've given you in this guide you can get an idea how expensive the stock is. The average is 15 - 25. So, if a companies P/E is below that, it tells you that company may be undervalued and is inexpensive compared to other stocks. However, if it is above that it may be a bit overpriced and has too much momentum. I would use this as a guide incorporated with all your other data and not P/E alone.

Return on Equity (ROE) - ROE is how much of a return the company is getting on the equity. This means how much money they are making with the money they have. In other words, it shows how well the company is using its equity. It is calculated by the formula Net Income / Equity. This is a great tool to compare stocks. Obviously the more return on equity the better. It's also great to see this ratio growing over time as well.

Debt to Asset Ratio - This ratio tells you how much debt they have in comparison to their assets (cash + property). Ideally the less debt, the better the company is doing. This is another great comparison tool to compare companies. A .6 debt ratio is considered high and 0 means they have no debt. I try to stick with companies with as little debt as possible.

There are more advanced ratios and chart analysis techniques, but you don't have to use them to get good results. These basic techniques have allowed me to beat the market and make significant gains for years. If you get started and love it, all those advanced techniques will be waiting once you've got the fundamentals down.

9 - A/B Test Your Companies

As with everything else, you're probably going to have winners and losers. Over time you'll see which ones are performing well and which ones are not. I always try to have 5 solid companies who are my core players and bring me in the money. I keep 5 - 10 stocks in my portfolio at any time. 5 of them are my winners and the others are my test companies.

Just like in marketing, you want to always be testing. A/B testing in marketing is a strategy in which you run 2 or more ads and find out which one gets the best results. I do pretty much the same thing with my stocks. I may buy 10 stocks and by the end of the year, I'll know which 5 are the winners and which 5 are the losers. I cut the losers, keep the winners, and then add 5 new companies to test them against my winners.

Once a year (sometimes more often), after running an A/B test on my stocks, I redraft new stocks. Just like in fantasy football in which new players are drafted each year for a new season, I do the same with my stocks. If you have a portfolio of 10 stocks. Drop the losing 5 and replace them with new winning stocks. Don't be afraid to drop the losers and keep the winners.

10 - Rebalance Every Year, There Can Be Too Much Of A Good Thing

Your winners are going to grow and sometimes they will grow big time. It's a good idea to rebalance your portfolio at least once a year. No one stock should exceed 20% of your portfolio. Say, for example, one of your winners is Apple. It may be growing faster than your others stocks and become 25% of your total stock portfolio. That's too much of your money in one stock.

Just like in fantasy football, if you're betting everything on one player and they get injured. You're in trouble. Don't bet everything on one stock. One big issue with that stock and it could wipe out a significant portion of your portfolio. At least once a year take some of those profits and invest in new stocks to try and keep a balanced portfolio of winners.

11 - Understand How A Recession Or Stock Correction Works To Reduce Emotion

Ok, guys, this is where most investors fail. Let's say you buy some stocks that you believe in and they're going up. You're making money! Suddenly, bad news comes out about economic or foreign policy and stocks start nosediving down. This is where a lot of investors screw up.

Their emotions say, PANIC! SELL, SELL, SELL! So they do. They sell their stock position and either take away a modest gain or a modest loss on that stock investment.

That is the path to mediocre returns or losses. You are not going to beat the stock market doing that. History is our best guide to predict how the stock market will react in the future. Yes, stocks go up and down. That is totally normal, but history shows the stocks move up and down while still moving upward on the trend line.

In other words, over the long term, the stock market always goes up. This makes long-term investing much safer and even easier to predict. Don't panic, stay calm!

Implement The Ultimate Investing Strategy

If you haven't already started, now is the time. Open your accounts, build your teams, and get ready to start building some serious wealth. This is the beginning of a very rich future for you. Don't drop the ball and ignore this secret. This secret is how so many people have become very wealthy! If you take action and do it, this will be an exciting and life-changing journey for you, just as it was for me!

Action Steps

Let's get you started investing!

-    Open a 401k

- Contribute at least 10% to your 401k

- Invest in Age Target Funds or a S&P 500 Index ETF in your 401k

- Open a IRA

- Contribute at least 5% to your IRA if you have a 401k, or 15% if you can't open a 401k

- Invest in Age Target Funds or a S&P 500 Index ETF in your IRA

- Open a stock investing account

- Contribute your 5% Emergency Fund savings once you have at least $1,000 in your savings account for your Emergency Fund

- Invest in stocks using the Ultimate Stock Investing Strategy

Secret #11 - Income Amplifier

Your job is not enough anymore. In fact, it's kind of risky to rely on only your job's income. Company loyalty is gone! We can't count on companies anymore to look out for us. It's actually the other way around. We have to watch out for them. We can't trust them to do what is best for us and our families.

Companies are greedy! Even if the CEO has the best intentions, they base their decisions on what makes the most profit for the company. That secures their job and ensures that the investors in the company are happy. If their goal is to obtain a certain amount of profit and the only way to hit that goal is to cut 50 jobs. That's what they're going to do.

Investors are after one thing, **PROFIT.** They're not there to ensure your family is secure or that you're living comfortably. It's truly sad, but this is how most companies work today:

- Investors own the companies.
- The CEO and executives work for the investors.
- The CEO and executives jobs are to squeeze out as much profit as possible for investors.

So where are we in that equation as the workers for these companies? We are the "labor," the "human resources." Management's job is to ensure that we are doing what is necessary to create the profit for the investors.

All the profit that we create simply goes to the investors and the executive's large salaries, bonuses, and stock options for creating that profit for them. Us "workers" are simply paid "market rate." In other words, we're paid the lowest rate we will accept as a group.

So for example, if they need someone to do accounting for them, they look for someone who has the knowledge and experience to get the job done at the lowest rate possible. If possible, they will hire an intern. If they need someone with a little more experience, they look for a young entry-level employee at the lowest rate possible and so on.

There's always a new, young, and inexperienced "worker" out there willing to take a low starting salary and this continues the cycle of keeping wages low for everyone.

Raises are becoming non-existent. 2% to 3% isn't a raise. It's simply the cost of living. This is economic inequality. This is today's job market. This is why you need multiple streams of income. It's time for us to take our future into our own hands and stop relying on companies to tell us how our future is going to turn out.

What Are Multiple Streams Of Income?

Well, to start, your job income is one source of income. Now, let's say you are married and your spouse also has a job, that's another source of income. You are now at 2 sources of income. That's a lot better than one, but don't stop there!

Unfortunately, that is where most people stop though... Most people get a job and then just accept what they're getting in their paycheck. This leads to bad or mediocre income at best. They just get too comfortable with their jobs and then they are stuck. They load up on debt and then are stuck at that job because they rely on their paychecks to pay down all that debt. Don't do it....

Instead, start creating a new source of income that is not your job. This gives you power! It gives you freedom! There really is nothing like the feeling of financial freedom. Let's say you are working for a company and they decide to make some changes that you don't like. That's, no problem if you have multiple streams of income. Just quit! You have the income coming in from another source to help sustain you while you search for a new job. That is the power of multiple sources of income.

Even better, over time your multiple sources of income may grow to the point that you don't even need to retain a job as a source of income. Wouldn't that be awesome!

This is the key to building wealth and financial freedom. The average millionaire has 7 sources of income! How many sources do you have right now? If you only have 1 or maybe 2, it's time to start working on creating your third source of income!

The Millionaire's 7 Streams Of Income

So how are these millionaires creating 7 streams of income? Well, each one is different and will have different types and amounts of income streams, but here are the most common streams of income for millionaires:

1 - Earned Income

This is where most people get their income. This is usually a job. You are trading your time for money.

2 - Profit Income

Profit Income comes from selling a product for more than it cost to buy it or make it. This is typically from starting some kind of business.

3 - Interest Income

The money you get from lending your money to someone else, a bank, or company.

4 - Dividend Income

Dividends usually come from owning stocks. Some companies you hold stock in pay out dividends to its investors.

5 - Rental Income

This type of income comes from owning a property and renting out portions or even all of it to renters.

6 - Capital Gains

Capital gains are the increase in the value of your portion of company ownership. This is generally gained by owning a stock that increases in value.

7 - Royalty Income

This is the most uncommon method of the 7, but basically, it is a situation where you own something like a piece of art, business, or intellectual property and sell the rights to another person. As they sell the items, you get a royalty from it.

Those are the 7 most common sources of income for millionaires, but I like to break it down into a much easier to understand method. I call it the Wealth Triad.

The Wealth Triad

The Wealth Triad is the 3 most common ways to build wealth. The most wealth you will gain will come from these 3 places:

- Owning a Business
- Real Estate
- Stock Investing

Notice, it's not coming from a job. Even high paying jobs like doctors or lawyers often don't generate as much wealth as someone who has wealth generated from one of these three sources.

So how do YOU start generating your own extra source of income from one of the wealth triad methods? I'll tell you how...

How You Can Create Multiple Sources Of Income

You probably have a job right now. Your paycheck is your first source of income. Maybe your significant other or spouse has a job as well. That's the second source of income. Maybe you have some other source that is your third. If not, you need to create your third. Take a look at the Wealth Triad and determine which route would fit you best. Here's a breakdown of the different methods:

Stock Investing

This is one of my favorite sources of income. You invest money in stocks and your stocks gain value, and maybe even create dividends for you. This is an awesome way to build wealth.

The downside is that stocks can be risky if you don't have the knowledge to invest well. Also, the growth can be slow in the beginning if you are starting with a small amount of money.

It's worth it though. The payoff can be huge. I never thought I would make the money I do today when I started stock investing. It's almost like a money tree that just keeps on giving! If you like analyzing numbers and companies, this might just be the perfect addition to your streams of income. Plus, you should already be on your way to investing in stocks with the Ultimate Investing Strategy.

Real Estate

Real Estate has been around forever and still remains one the best ways to build wealth and generate income. There are lots of ways to make money in real estate.

You could:

- Rent a room in your home with Airbnb
- Rent a house or multifamily property
- Flip a house (buy it, renovate it, and sell it for a profit)
- The possibilities can be endless with real estate.

I've owned several rental properties in my life and I even flipped one property. It's hard work, but if real estate is your thing, there is definitely potential to create a brand new income stream with it.

Owning a Business

Starting a business is probably the most common method people try when attempting to create another source of income. A business can be hard to get started, but they are so rewarding when they work. Making money on your own by providing a product or service to others is exhilarating and freeing.

I highly suggest starting a small side business. Don't try to go to the extreme of starting a brick and mortar business like a restaurant for example. Start with a side hustle. Starting a business is a huge undertaking and trying to eat the whole elephant will just stress you out and generally get you nowhere.

Identify your skills and passions and start a side hustle to learn how to run a business before taking it to the next level. Here are some side hustle ideas you could start quickly:

- Sell a product on Etsy.

- Landscaping/mowing for neighborhoods around your house.
- Start a family photography business where you go to their homes or to beautiful parks.
- Create a eBook about something you have skills in and sell it to others who want to learn those skills (kinda like this book :))

These few examples are easy to start and don't take much investment up front. There are lots of side hustle opportunities out there you could start in no time and if they work you can scale them up to become a huge income generating machine. Any of these methods can create an awesome income stream and once you have multiple streams it opens your minds to the possibilities.

The Freedom of Multiple Income Streams

The lie we've been fed since we were kids about getting a job and working until your 65 is BS. There's a better way to live. A way to live where you're not trapped by your job and reliant on them for your own financial success.

Millionaires on average have 7 streams of income. How many streams do you have now? Choose a new stream that you want to explore and dig in. Learn about it and take action. Once you have a few income streams, the power leans into your favor. You're no longer reliant on a job for all of your income and soon enough those extra income streams may exceed your job income and you may decide to drop the job altogether. Thats what financial freedom is.

Multiple Income Streams = Financial Freedom

Create a new income stream today to get on the path to financial freedom and your life will change forever.

How To Increase Your Income Right Now

Now, your mind is probably is spinning with possible income stream ideas, but before you begin building those new income streams, let's look at how you can increase your income right now at your first income stream, your 9 - 5 job.

Review Your Paycheck

First off, let's look at your paycheck and see if we can amplify it right now. This secret made me an extra $200 every 2 weeks! Our paychecks are usually just a percentage of what we really earn. Taxes take a huge chunk of your pay along with all kinds of little deductions.

When was the last time you took a good look at your pay stub and made sure you're not paying for crap you don't really need? When was the last time you checked to make sure you're not overpaying on your taxes? If you're like most people it's probably been a long time or possibly, you've never done it at all.

I'm going to show you how to do a spring cleaning on your paycheck and possibly give yourself a big raise! Pull up your last paycheck and take a look at what you could change. Take a look at all those deductions coming out. Let's go through them to see if you are overpaying or simply paying for things you really don't need. It's very possible you have money just waiting to be grabbed and with a simple change you could be pocketing a lot more money each paycheck.

Review Your Federal Tax Deductions On Your Paycheck

This is a big one. This is an area where a lot of people are overpaying and can make a big change to your paycheck.

In fact, this is where I increased my paycheck big time ($200) just by making a simple change!

Do you get a large refund during tax season each year? If you do, you're paying the IRS too much money. Any extra money you pay them is a tax free loan to the IRS. Who wants to pay them extra? Especially for free? The IRS provides a handy little calculator that can help you determine how much you should be paying in federal taxes on your paychecks.

Goto https://apps.irs.gov/app/withholdingcalculator/ and fill out the fields to find out how much you should be withholding and then come back. At the end of the calculator they will tell you how many allowances you should be taking.

Now, take a look at your most recent paycheck. How many Federal Exemptions / Allowances do you have on there? The lower the number, the more they take out of your paycheck and send to the IRS. So if the recommended number from the calculator is higher than the number on your paycheck, you're sending too much money to the IRS.

Contact your HR department and have that changed. This will increase your pay on your next paycheck and all paychecks going forward. This is exactly how I increased my paycheck by $200!

Now, you will get less money back when you file your taxes, but it's usually better for most people to have that money throughout the year rather than waiting until once a year to get your money. The #1 complaint I hear from people is that they just don't have enough money day to day. You have to decide whether that money would be more valuable to have now and every month going forward or just in February tax return season.

Also, verify that your Taxable Marital Status is correct. If you're married then change it too married and if you're single make sure it says single. This affects your taxes significantly.

Review Your Insurance Deductions On Your Paycheck

There seems to be an insurance for everything these days. Dog insurance, house insurance, disability insurance, dental insurance, life insurance, car insurance, etc.. You name it, there's an insurance for it. Is all this really necessary? Sometimes it is, but not always.

It's best to take an analytical approach to insurance. I personally only have a high deductible health insurance plan and a dental plan coming out of my paychecks.

List out all of the insurance payments you have coming out. Do you really need all of them? Just to give you an example. I don't take vision insurance because I'd pay out more to the insurance than I would just getting an annual exam for $80. Now, if you pay a lot for vision expenses, then maybe its worth it.

I do have dental insurance because my family has lots of teeth work to do and the discounts from the insurance plan make it worthwhile to have the plan because the cost of the insurance premiums are less than the cost of the dental work I have to pay for.

Take some time and do the homework to decide if you really need all of those insurances. Don't just buy insurance because it's available. Only buy it if you really believe the cost of the premiums would be worth it.

Review The Additional "Benefits" On Your Paycheck

What else is coming out of your paycheck? Companies come up with the weirdest things to call "benefits." Other than taxes, health insurance, and dental insurance, the only other thing coming out of my paycheck is my Roth 401k deposits and my HSA deposits. That's all I have coming out. I try to keep these reoccurring payments out of my paycheck as much as possible. It's amazing how fast your paycheck can be drained with these deductions!

Take a hard look at everything coming out of your paycheck and ask yourself, is it really worth it?

How To Increase Your Pay Right Now

Most people could be making more money at their job right now. When you get a job, you have to have the dreaded salary negotiation. Most people don't even negotiate, so they start below what they really could be getting. On top of that, many people stay for years without switching jobs.

This leads to the terrible "merit" increases. This is simply a 2% to 3% raise which is really just covering inflation. It's not a real raise. The majority of companies are not giving out raises voluntarily anymore. Don't let a company push you around. You are in control of your pay. I'll show you how to take control of your own career.

Switch Jobs Every 1 - 3 Years Unless You Love Your Current Company

It pays to switch jobs every 1 to 3 years. It's very common to get 10% + increases in pay when you move to a new job, but if you were to stay at the same company you'll likely get a 2 - 3% raise.

Now, if you really love your company or your current job, that's cool. Stay right where you are, but continue on to find out how to increase you income right now in your current position.

How To Request A Raise And Get It

If you've worked in your current role 1 to 3 years or even more and have performed well, you most likely could get an increase in your income right now. To do this you will need to either email or setup a 1 on 1 meeting with your manager depending on what is normal for your company and manager or simply what feels best for you.

Next, it's time to get prepared. No matter if you're emailing or meeting with your manager, you need to sit down and write a letter to your manager. You'll be able to email it if you choose that route, otherwise you will need to study it for your meeting. Here's what you'll need to put in it:

Intro

Tell your manager upfront what you are requesting. Tell them how much of a raise you deserve and that you will explain why. I'll show you how to determine how much you should be getting paid soon.

Current Level

Describe your current pay rate and what role you are in.

Increase In Responsibility

Describe the additional responsibilities you have taken on since you began working in this role.

Increase In Experience

How has your experience increased since you began your role? How many years of experience do you now have versus when you started?

Increase In Education, Certifications, Or Trainings

Have you completed new training, completed a certification, or completed more formal education? If so, how have you implemented what you have learned in your role?

Positive Performance Reviews

Describe the positive performance reviews you have received since you began working in your role.

How You Have Helped The Company

What have you done in your role that has had a positive impact at the company? Be specific. For example,

"I have completed XYZ project which has increased company revenue by $100,000 per year."

This could be a task or project that led to an increase of revenue, decrease in expenses, more efficient process, etc.

Here is a template:

"I (POSITIVE ACTION) that has helped the company by (POSITIVE RESULT)."

This part is very important. It shows explicitly how you are helping the company and gives them a real reason to justify your pay increase.

Market Value

Next, you'll need to review around 3 salary sites to determine what the market value of your position is based off of your location, certifications, education, and number of years of experience. This is how you will know how much pay you should be getting.

Some popular resources are Indeed and Salary. Take a screenshot of the Market Values and place it in your email if you are emailing the letter or print it out if you are meeting with your manager. Ask for the median value and even higher if you can provide examples of how you have specifically helped the company in the previous section.

Conclusion

Wrap up your request again with what you are asking for and summarize the reasons why from the previous sections. I have used this exact outline to ask for and receive raises many times throughout my career and you can do it as well.

Action Steps

If you follow these steps, you will drastically amplify your income from your job and your new income streams. It's time to start making more money. As you make more money, you will be able to save more, invest more, and reach financial freedom much earlier.

- Choose a new income stream and get started on building it
- Review your paycheck to increase your 9 - 5 income
- Prepare your pay increase request and present it to your manager
- If you've been at your job for more than 3 years and don't love it, begin to look for a new job

Secret #12 - Money Automation Blueprint

I use to suck with money. Like, really suck at it. That is no joke. When I graduated college I was struggling. (Even though I graduated with a Bachelor's degree in Accounting and Finance…) I fell into the usual debt traps that most of us millennials do. Maybe you're in this boat too.

I knew I had to fix it, so I starting reading every book on personal finance, making money, and investing I could get my hands on. I implemented a lot of changes in my finances as you've seen throughout this book, but the #1 thing that helped me turn it around was automating my money. The Money Automation Blueprint is the step-by-step process I took to automate my money. Now that I've documented it for you, you can implement it in your life too.

Imagine if you had a personal assistant managing your money for you. They pay your bills, set aside money for investing, save money for your next vacation, and tell you how much money you can safely spend on fun things without messing everything up. That's what money automation does for you. In this secret, I'll show you how to automate your money from start to finish so you can sit back, relax, and enjoy life like you should! Not only does it make life better, but it's essential for managing your money.

Have you ever tried running or working out every day after not doing it for a long time? How did it go? If you're anything like me, it's sooo hard to build that habit and do it consistently. Things come up, I forget, sometimes I just don't feel like it. Managing your money successfully works the same way. You could say to yourself today, I'm going to manage my money like a badass and begin saving money tomorrow! How will it go? Maybe you'll make some progress, but most of the time it will just drop off and you'll be right back where you started.

There is a way to beat that problem. You probably guessed it! You have to automate your money! With exercising you can't automate your workouts but thankfully with money you can automate it. This is the secret to success with money! Yes, your about to learn the #1 secret to becoming rich and handling your money like a badass! With automation, your money just works for you. You don't even have to think about it, or even remember to do certain financial tasks on certain days. It's chugging along in the background making you richer every year.

So how you implement this amazing automation secret? I'm going to show you step by step how to do it right now.

Automate Your Income Streams With Direct Deposit

If you don't have a bank account you need to get one. Once you have a bank account, you need to make sure every income stream is setup to go straight into your bank account via direct deposit. There are some exceptions, but most modern employers can send your paychecks and other income directly to your bank account just by filling out a simple form.

If you have other income like government payments, they can also direct deposit into your bank account. It's simply a matter of filling out a form. If you have income streams from sources like PayPal or Stripe, those should also be direct deposited directly into your bank account. Bottom line, every income source should be automatically going into your checking account as it comes in. It's an easy first step and quick win!

Automate Your Insurance Payments

If you work for a company you most likely have insurance through them. Make sure any insurance related expenses are coming out automatically from your paychecks from your employer.

- Health Insurance
- Dental Insurance
- Vision Insurance
- Disability Insurance

Whatever type of insurance you use or need, make sure to send the payment directly to them from you paychecks so you don't have to deal with it. Talk to your **HR** department if they are not being automatically paid. No thinking about it, no worrying about it being paid. You see the pattern?

So far, your income is automated into your checking account. Your insurance payments are automated and we're just getting started!

Automate Your Money Snapshot

Tracking your money and net worth can be done with paper and pen, but once you've mastered the process, it's time to automate it. The Money Snapshot is your dashboard for your financial life. Imagine if your money dashboard is automatically updating for you. It's completely possible with the right tools.

My absolute favorite tool for creating my Money Snapshot is Personal Capital. With Personal Capital you can automatically pull in transactions and balances from all your financial accounts. (Most of them, there are some accounts that won't integrate with Personal Capital unfortunately)

You'll connect your bank accounts, physical assets, debts, investments, and any other financial accounts you have and then Personal Capital will do the heavy lifting. It will connect to those accounts and update your balances for you so you don't have to. This is an example of just some the magic of money automation with technology.

Your Net Worth will also be automatically calculated for you on the fly. This gives you a real time picture of your finances at any time. You can't beat it. All you have to do is the initial connection and then you will have an automated money dashboard to get an understanding of your money at a glance! That is an automated Money Snapshot!

Even though it's automated, don't forgot to monitor it like I talked about in Secret #5. Schedule 1 day per month on you calendar to review your Money Snapshot.

Automate Your Perfect Budget

There is a TON of budgeting software out there. Apps, software, web apps, etc. I've tried a lot of different ones but for me that absolute best budgeting software has always been You Need a Budget. The only downside to You Need a Budget is the fact that it costs an annual fee. If you can afford it and are really serious about automating your money. This is the app to get it. It truly is a great budgeting app.

They have a software version, a web version, and even an app version so you can take your budget with you anywhere. You Need a Budget automatically connects to your checking account and even your credit card accounts to pull in all your transactions and apply them to your budget categories! This is how it automates your budget. You simply have to review the transactions to verify they were categorized correctly.

I highly recommend checking out this app, it can be a game changer in your finances. If you don't have the money to spend on YNAB, take a look at Mint. It's similar but not as robust. Best of all it's free!

Make sure you are scheduling a day each week to review your budget transaction to keep it running smoothly.

Automate Your Perfect Budget Financial Goals

You should have financial goals in your Perfect Budget. It could be as simple as saving for a home down payment or it could be something as cool as a trip to Hawaii. No matter what your financial goals are, the easiest way to achieve them is to automate the process of saving towards your goal. Maybe you want to go to Las Vegas in 1 year.

No problem, figure out how much the trip would cost and then divide that number by 12. (12 months in a year)

Here is an example:

Let's say I want to go to Las Vegas in a year. I think the total cost of hotel, airfare, food, Uber, etc will be about $2,000. To reach this goal in a year I divide 2,000 / 12 = $167 per month. So, now I know I need to setup an automatic transfer in my bank to a savings account for $167 every month on the 15th for example. You could even make it even smaller amounts if that works better for you. For example, you could divide $167 by 4 and that would be $42 per week.

There is also apps like Digit that can help you save towards your goal if you'd prefer to not do it with your bank. As long as it's automated and you don't even have to think about it, it will be SO MUCH EASIER! Automate those goals and your chance of reaching your financial goals will be so much better.

Automate Your Bills And Debt

Automating your bills is going to make a huge change in your life. Bills are painful to deal with. Mentally, you're watching all of you hard earned money go out the door. It's just plain stressful. It takes time away from you that you could be doing something else. Thankfully, it doesn't have to be this way. You can automate your bills and hardly even have to think about them. Here's my favorite technique for automating my bills so that I don't even miss the money and it allows me to spend only about 15 minutes a month working on my bills.

List out all of your bills and how much they are on average. Assign each bill to a paycheck. Try to distribute the bills evenly so that you have remaining money from your paycheck after each bill is paid.

To give you an example, here is how I pay my bills monthly:

Secret #12 - Money Automation Blueprint

I get 2 paychecks per month. I assign 2 bills to 1 paycheck and 3 bills to other paycheck.

As soon as that paycheck hits my bank account, the assigned bills are scheduled to be paid from my bank account immediately through my banks scheduled payments feature. The money comes out as soon as I get paid so that I never even miss the money and I don't have to stress out about paying the bills and watching that money go out. I no longer have to worry about my bills. I just do a quick checkup every month to make sure everything is working as intended. It's that easy.

This is where you can automate your debt as well. It's the perfect way to get out of debt. Automating your debt reduces so much stress! You're going to love it. This works exactly like how you automated your bills. Take your list of debt payments from your Debt Elimination Plan and assign them to your paychecks. Next, you'll need to setup an automatic reoccurring payment for each debt. That's it! This strategy is so simple, yet so powerful. This will allow you to pay down your debt without worrying about. It will be automatically paid in the fastest method possible.

You will need to review your bills and debt payments once a month to make sure the automations are working. If you payoff a debt you will also need to revisit your Debt Elimination Plan to adjust it as you payoff your debts.

Automate Your Savings Roadmap

An emergency fund is critical to make your money work for you. The idea is that you create a separate fund at your bank that allows you to aside money in the case of an emergency. Instead of reaching for a credit card, you can use your own money in those situations where you have an unexpected expense that you just don't have enough money for.

Create a separate account that you can easily transfer money from and to your checking account. Setup an automatic transfer on a weekly or monthly schedule to your emergency fund ideally around the time of your paycheck deposit so that you don't even realize the money is gone. Once it's setup, you don't have to worry about it and the next time you have an unexpected expense you'll have a nice chunk of money sitting there waiting for you!

There are also apps out there that can do this for you as well like Digit and Acorns if you prefer using an app.

Once you've reached $1,000 in your Emergency Fund it's time to start putting any new Emergency Fund savings money into a better investment account which I'll show you next.

Automate Your Ultimate Investing Strategy

One of the keys to investing is automation. Allowing your money to automatically invest for you takes out a lot of the emotion that causes many investors too fail. Automation truly is what makes investing work. By not having to think about it, you'll be investing automatically without the stress of forgetting or worrying about the money. Let's take out that emotion and automate your investments.

Your employer probably has a retirement account option like a 401k. Hopefully you're enrolled in it if they do. Most employees automatically deduct a contribution to your 401k from your paycheck and may even contribute some for you. If you're not automatically depositing in your companies retirement account you need to. Setup an automatic transfer into your company 401k.

You may also have a IRA. You probably can't get your IRA through your company so you will have to have this automatically withdrawn from your checking account to your IRA provider. Contact your IRA provider or just login to the online site for your IRA and setup an automatic transfer to your IRA from your bank account. Scheduling this takes all of the willpower issues out of the equation and makes savings for your retirement effortless.

Finally, if you are investing in a stock account like Robinhood. Setup an automatic deposit into your stock account. You'll have to choose the investments, but that's what secret #10 is all about.

This step alone will help you build wealth without thinking about it while doing whatever you love!

Monitor Your Automations

To make sure your automations continue to work, you will need to do some monitoring. While automation covers 90% of the work for you, money automation is never 100% automated. You have to keep an eye on your money to make sure everything is running smoothly.

Create a financial habits checklist to keep your automation on track. You'll use this checklist to review your automated systems to make sure everything is working as you intended. You may not be able to get your money 100% automated, but 90% is way better than 0%.

Here's what you need to be watching:

- Review your Money Snapshot monthly
- Review your Bills and Debt Elimination Plan monthly
- Review your Savings & Investments monthly
- Review your Perfect Budget weekly

Let's Automate Your Money

Pretty much everything about your money can be automated and the more you automate your money, the better it will work for you. No more thinking about your money constantly, worrying about it, or wasting time managing it when it could all be automated. Automate your money today and find out just how easy managing your money can be!

Action Steps

Let's automate your money!

- Automate your income streams with direct deposits
- Automate your insurance payments
- Automate your Money Snapshot
- Automate your Perfect Budget
- Automate your Bills And Debt Elimination Plan
- Automate your Savings Roadmap
- Automate your Ultimate Investing Strategy
- Review your Money Snapshot monthly
- Review your Bills and Debt Elimination Plan monthly
- Review your Savings & Investments monthly
- Review your Perfect Budget weekly

Conclusion

Congratulations! You've learned the Financial Freedom Secrets and are implementing them in your own life! It's not over though! Keep learning and never stop! Head over to my website to stay current with the ever-changing world of money at moneybadass.co.

—Dave Shepherd from Money Badass

Bonus Materials

I've created a bonus resource site where you can access spreadsheets, frameworks, and more. This will help you succeed so I highly suggest signing up for it now. Inside you'll find all the resources organized by each of the secrets in this book making it super easy to use! I'll be adding more content over time so make sure you get free instant access right now!

Visit the following link to get free access to your Financial Freedom Secrets bonus materials now:

https://moneybadass.teachable.com/courses/financial-freedom-secrets

www.ingramcontent.com/pod-product-compliance
Lightning Source LLC
Chambersburg PA
CBHW021404210526
45463CB00001B/217